Nahal Tajadod was born in Tehran and moved to France in 1971. She has written several books about China and a fictional biography of the Persian poet, Roumi.

Also by Nahal Tajadod

Roumi, le brûlé

Tehran, Lipstick and Loopholes

NAHAL TAJADOD

Translated by Adriana Hunter

virago

VIRAGO

First published in Great Britain in 2010 by Virago Press
This paperback edition published in 2011 by Virago Press
Reprinted 2011

Copyright © Nahal Tajadod 2010

The moral right of the author has been asserted.

A CIP catalogue record for this book
is available from the British Library.

ISBN 978-1-84408-514-9

Typeset in Bembo by M Rules
Printed and bound in Great Britain by
Clays Ltd, St Ives plc

Papers used by Virago are from well-managed forests
and other responsible sources.

MIX
Paper from
responsible sources
FSC® C104740

Virago Press
An imprint of
Little, Brown Book Group
100 Victoria Embankment
London EC4Y 0DY

An Hachette UK Company
www.hachette.co.uk

www.virago.co.uk

Saturday

I was born in this place, I know Tehran, I've got friends here. Soon I'll have to head back to Paris, where I live. My return ticket, with Iran Air, is ready. One slight concern, nothing really: I need to renew my Iranian passport.

I'm used to it. It normally takes three days. I've got ten days to spare: that's more than enough.

To renew my passport I have to get, amongst other things, Islamic-style ID photos: no hair appearing beneath the scarf, no visible make-up, no smile. Basically you have to produce a picture of a woman looking straight at the lens when, in her day-to-day life, she isn't allowed to look men in the eye.

In order to compose a photograph like this – and it really is a composition, not a snapshot – I absolutely have to find a professional photographer. They're used to this sort of exercise: they have at their disposal a range of thick plain scarves, make-up remover for eyes and lips, and a long coat with a collar that buttons right up, in other words all the paraphernalia needed to transform an ordinary woman – whatever length her hair, however much make-up she's wearing, and whether she's wearing a print dress or jeans and a T-shirt – into an Islamic woman.

The way an Islamic woman looks has been carefully thought out. It means something: the veil covering her head represents martyrs' blood shed during the Iran–Iraq war (more than a million dead on the Iranian side); the buttons on her collar, pressing on her throat and choking her slightly, are an allusion to the healthy state of her husband's or brother's honour, for the simple reason that those buttons ensure no one can see her female flesh.

Before going to one of these photo studios – I can think of a couple not far from home – I take the precaution of not reapplying my lipstick in case the photographers are short of lotion, and I choose a black scarf and crinkle-effect blouse with a high collar, bought at Pleats in Paris. The design doesn't reveal, or even suggest, a single bodily curve because it drowns the bust under swathes of pleated polyester. In Iran very few people know the designer Issey Miyake, and covering up with one of his ample garments can't betray the least sartorial affectation, which might be seen as questionable.

Still, I do decide to put on a bit of perfume. A glance at my dressing table and I choose Santa Maria Novella's Rose. Perhaps I'm secretly hoping that, thanks to my perfume and the unsuspected elegance of my top, I might be able to contaminate the Islamic prototype with a bit of womanliness thanks to a few subtle, invisible and undetectable hints of Japan and Florence.

I go out and, after a few minutes' hesitant walk along collapsing pavements punctuated with electrical cables, I catch sight of the two photo studios. They're not far apart. One is named after Mehdi, the hidden Imam, the one who disappeared down a well long ago, and whose return has been solemnly awaited by fervent Shiites for twelve centuries.

The other studio is called Ecbatana, the name of the ancient capital of the Achaemenid sovereigns who built Persepolis. I choose the second. Before the Islamic Revolution I wouldn't have minded which one I went to and might even have opted for the first, in recognition of one of my cousins whose name is Mehdi. Now I choose the greatest antiquity, the illustrious heyday of Persia.

I stop in front of the Ecbatana studio's window display and read the words written on the glass: WE CAN FILM AND PHOTOGRAPH ALL YOUR SPECIAL OCCASIONS. This instantly reminds me of an acquaintance of ours, the son of a social-climbing upstart from the north of Iran, who had his father's funeral filmed by a professional director. The tape was handed round the family until the first anniversary of the death, when the rich young orphan hired a giant screen in the gardens of the family home and projected the film of the ceremony, now edited and set to *Für Elise*.

Black clothes, black gladioli, black hangings: it looked like the reverse of a wedding. Not that the young man was particularly sensitive to the memory of this funeral but, to display his fortune, he had chosen to show off the burial of the man who probably handed it down to him: his father.

As I glance at the photos dressing the shop front, I see a bridegroom in profile, with slicked back hair, plucked eyebrows and a touched-up nose modelled on Brad Pitt's. In a manicured hand with a hint of nail polish, he is holding a bouquet of white roses towards an absent bride. You see, current law forbids displaying photos of women in any kind of shop window, so those white roses are destined for no one.

In the next picture another groom is opening the door of a Mercedes decorated with flowers and ribbons, to reveal a silhouette that I can only assume is his betrothed although all I can make out are her feet, just touching the ground and crammed into tight shoes with stiletto heels. I spend a long time looking at this picture which strikes me as slightly subversive. The Islamic powers actually forbid women wearing high heels because the clicking of a woman's heels as she walks could always arouse a good Muslim, therefore provoking dangerous sensations.

For a moment I picture Wall Street with its hundreds of women in court shoes running in every direction, blissfully unaware that they are unleashing better erections in New York brokers than Viagra can produce. I can't take my eyes off those satin shoes in the Mercedes, the only evidence that there is a woman on the far side of the door. They remind me of ones I've bought myself or have been given by other people, but have never worn because they're too tight. The invisible bride must have been given them — these abbreviated shoes — as a present, probably from her future sister-in-law who'd just got back from a trip to Dubai or somewhere else.

Ah, Dubai and the Iranian middle class! For the last fifteen years all that Iranians can dream about is spending long weekends (from Wednesday evening to Friday evening) in the highly concreted paradise that is Dubai. Getting there doesn't require endless insurmountable procedures at the consulate to obtain a visa, or knowledge of English, German or Swedish. Most of the shops are run by fellow-countrymen who have fled the Islamic regime, and Persian is spoken and heard everywhere. Even if a situation means you really have to use the Arab language, whole chunks of Muslim prayers can come to your aid at any time. *Allah akbar* (God is great), for instance, can help indicate astonishment at some monument, such as the Burj al-arab; *al hamdollah* (thanks be to God), is freely used as any expression of gratitude; *serat al-mostaghim* (the path of righteousness) to point the way to a taxi driver, and so on. Prayer is a tremendous help to tourists.

People who grow rich in Tehran eagerly spend their money on the beaches of Dubai, in their swimming costumes, with a glass of whisky in their hand and a horizon full of high-rise buildings behind them. Here their lucky wives can go out without Islamic scarves, aerating their fake blonde hair to the whims of the wind, the hot wind of the Arabian desert, even strolling about the foyers of large hotels in shorts and blouses, and bringing home gifts for cousins less blessed by fate or for future brides: shoes that are always too tight.

That's where I abandon the invisible bride's stilettos which have taken me all the way to Dubai, not without a fleeting thought for the European fetish for shoes and for Catherine Deneuve's patent-clad foot, dressed by Roger Vivier, silently climbing the stairs in the brothel for the first time in *Belle de jour*.

Further along the window I notice a picture of a little girl of six or seven, certainly less than nine – the age of puberty for girls. She's blowing towards a candle on a birthday cake cut into four pieces, each bearing one of the letters of the word LOVE. The child in the photo is wearing more make-up than a chorus girl at the Moulin Rouge. The sequins stuck round her eyes, the silvery powder on her hair and the red of her nails bring me out in goose pimples. Her puckered lips miming blowing out the candle (egged on by her mother, she must have re-enacted the gesture a dozen times for the purposes of the picture) could teach the most experienced porn actress a thing or two about simulated desire and fake longing. By exhibiting her like this, before she was old enough for enforced scarf-wearing, her mother must have been transferring her own thwarted dreams on to her offspring.

The photographer waves me in: *befarmayin, befarmayin.*

I step into the shop where, as everywhere, portraits of the Ayatollah Khomeyni and the current Supreme Guide Ayatollah Khameneyi have pride of place. When I explain that I've come for passport photos the man tells me his colleague, who actually takes the pictures, will be back in a few minutes. I deduce that he won't be back for at least an hour and immediately regret choosing the Ecbatana studio and not the Mehdi. I try to leave with the excuse that in the meantime I need to go to an electrical repairman with my hairdryer which I'm lugging round in a basket bought at Aigues-Mortes in France.

'Your hairdryer's broken?' he asks, using the informal you-form everyone seems to employ since the Islamic Republic was established.

'Yes.'

'And how did it happen?'

I reply without thinking, 'Yesterday evening, when I started drying my hair after my bath, it just suddenly stopped. That's all.'

'Have you got it with you?'

'The hairdryer? Yes.'

'Can I see it?'

'Of course.'

I open my French basket. He takes the contraption in his pudgy hands, looks at it for a moment, takes a screwdriver from a drawer in the store room and immediately attacks the beast. He is short, limp, almost bald, aged between thirty and thirty-five, and wearing a gold chain round his neck. I now realise it's too late, I've just made a mistake, and won't get out of his studio for hours. The little man spreads the entrails of my Babyliss 2300W before me with meticulous care.

'Don't worry, it'll only take five minutes,' he says.

Why didn't I choose the Mehdi studio? They wouldn't have talked to me in that familiar you-form, they wouldn't have dissected my hairdryer to kill time, keeping me pinioned in their shop waiting for a photographer.

I'm about to leave, almost prepared to give up on my Babyliss, when the door bursts open and the photographer we've been waiting for comes in. Now, he's more on the good-looking side. He has lots of thick hair storming about his face. With one eye still on my Babyliss in its component pieces, I tell him I'm here for a passport photo.

'Very good,' he says, 'this way.'

He uses both his hands to push back his mass of hair, and points me towards a darkened corner. Several Islamic coats are hanging on the wall and I notice scarves and bottles of make-up and make-up remover on a table. The photographer points out that the mascaras, hairbrushes and blushers are for Iranian clients dealing with foreign consulates or who live in Europe or the US. They make the most of Iran's highly competitive rates to have a whole selection of portraits done to hand out to foreign universities, police headquarters and whoever asks for them.

The photographer points at a beige coat and advises me to put it on because my blouse strikes him as too creased. I restrain myself from telling him about Issey Miyake's famous pleats and do as I'm told. As I put the coat on I try not to inhale the smell that I imagine is impregnated in it, the smell of *shanbelileh*, a herb found exclusively in Iran which, when used in cooking, only leaves the eater's body after days and days of washing. Half of Iran is steeped in this smell, the other half in the reek of petrol.

Since childhood I haven't been able to bear the smell of *shanbelileh*. I put the coat on and, just as I feared, recognise exhalations of the wretched plant. I throw the garment down on a chair and explain to the photographer that my ruffled blouse won't 'ruffle' the authorities at the Ministry of the Interior, that I'd prefer to stick to it and he can start getting his equipment ready.

'Very well,' he says.

He leads me to the studio, adjusts the height of the seat, goes round behind the camera, comes back out and, with a finger that smells of cigarettes, rubs away the subtle traces of my lipstick and zips my blouse up further. Then he holds my chin still and runs his hand under my scarf to tuck away a rebellious lock of hair. What sort of verdict would a doctor of religion reach confronted with this situation: a woman alone with a stranger in a dark room, letting him stroke her lips, her neck, her chin and her hair without saying a word?

'Hell in the next world, prison in this one,' the learned soul would reply.

The photographer opens the door to the changing area. He can't bear the rose-scented perfume I'm wearing, it reminds him too much of mosques and cemeteries, he tells me. I think of the thousands of hours invested by monks and nuns at the Officina de Santa Maria Novella in Florence, only for their fragrance to end up being compared to the smell of Muslim cemeteries. All my efforts are

falling flat. Neither the Pleats blouse, the Santa Maria
Novella Rose nor even my Dries Van Noten pumps succeed in impressing the photographer. I look at the lens
without smiling and hold my breath. He takes the picture.

When we come out of the studio the Babyliss is still
completely dismantled on the counter. The little salesman
reassures me once again: I can come back to pick up the
photos and the hairdryer that same evening. Everything
will be ready.

My mobile suddenly rings. A call from Paris. I answer in
French and now, for the first time, I make an impression.
All of a sudden they stop using the informal form of
address. After a moment's silence the salesman and the
photographer, Hassan and Morad (those are the names
they call each other), offer me a chair and a cup of tea. I
want to pay and leave, but they insist. In the end the two
men confide in me with their hopes: what they really want
is to go somewhere – anywhere – in Europe. In order to
achieve this they have to fill in a request for a Schengen
visa. Hassan opens his briefcase and hands me two forms in
Swedish. I tell them I don't speak Swedish, can't read the
form and am even less equipped to fill it in.

'Write in French, it doesn't matter,' they reply.

I pick up my pen and fill in the boxes for their names.
I ask them for their dates of birth using Christian dating.
Morad runs his hands through his long hair in a gesture
that is clearly quite a habit and admits that he doesn't
know it. Neither does Hassan. They don't have their
passports on them. They announce that they will bring
them to my house that evening with the photos and the
hairdryer.

'I have to go out with my husband this evening,' I say.

I feel they're on to my subterfuge straight away because

they point out that they could leave the package with a neighbour or with the caretaker in my building.

'You could just fill in the forms tomorrow morning and slip them under the shop door. Whenever suits you.'

Now I'm feeling reassured: I won't have to see them again. I agree and take the forms.

'How much do I owe you?' I eventually ask, purse in hand.

Speaking in unison, they refuse any payment point blank, either for the photos or the hairdryer which is still in pieces at the moment. When I insist, they decline my offer again:

'No, no, you don't owe us anything.'

I persevere. Still in vain. In the end I give in. I know that there are limits even to Iranian *tarof*, the affectation of refusing out of politeness the things you most want: at a dinner party, for example, when someone offers you another helping and you're dying to have some, you say no, no thank you and no again. I understand that I mustn't press my point and that, in their way, the photographers are sincere in their refusal. It's part of their upbringing and their customs.

'Why do you want to leave Iran?' I ask before going out.

Once again Morad sweeps his hair off his forehead with both hands, then looks right at me with his black eyes with their interminable lashes and, without raising his voice, says:

'Iran is a cage.'

Without replying I close the door of the shop on them.

Back at home I proudly open my diary to strike through the reminders *Get passport photos* and *Repair hairdryer*, only to wonder whether the gesture is altogether valid. At the moment I don't actually have the pictures or the hairdryer.

*

A little later the caretaker calls me on the videophone. The device, like the building, dates back to the late 1970s. At the time an apartment with a videophone was very chic and up to the minute. Nowadays you can't get the spare parts for the thing anywhere, either in Iran or in France, and if you inadvertently have the misfortune to look at the image, a pale, rectangular, rather frightening black and white form appears, the sort make-up artists for science fiction films should consult for inspiration.

Still, I do recognise something on the videophone's small screen: a black horizontal bar cutting the shapeless image in two. It's the caretaker, all right. Like all Kurds, he wears a thick Stalin moustache, and that's what I recognise. He tells me he's coming up to deliver a package dropped off by two men.

Mr Eskandari, our caretaker, has lost all contact with one of his sons in Sweden. Having set off, theoretically, to study or work in Stockholm, his son then joined the Swedish branch of the People's Mujahedeen, an armed resistance movement, and never sent news again. What happened to him? No one knows. Mr Eskandari has asked every inhabitant in the building who has been to Sweden to look for his son's name in the phone book there.

Mr Eskandari believes, probably with good reason, that his son fell foul of the movement's leaders and was liquidated by them. He consoles himself for this disappearance with the thought that hundreds of thousands of young men also lost their lives on the Iran–Iraq front, but that doesn't stop his eyes shining with a distinctive light whenever he hears someone's going to Sweden.

He rings the bell. My door is always open. I can never

actually close it, still imagining I'm in our old house where the front door opened into a garden. Mr Eskandari comes in and hands me the package, and I see his expression brighten with the same tenacious hope revived every time a trip to Sweden is mentioned. I promise to ask the photographers to do everything they can to track down the missing son once they have been given their visas. He puts his hand in his pocket and takes out a tired, worn piece of paper folded in four, the same one he shows to anyone heading for Stockholm. As his slender tapering fingers glide over a series of numbers almost erased by the passage of time, he tells me they could try ringing this number. I copy it out – as I already have in the past – and reassure him as best I can, quoting the verse announcing that Jacob's son Joseph has returned to Canaan after many years' absence.

We both know his son is dead.

Mr Eskandari goes back down to the ground floor. He walks, as all Kurds do, very upright, almost haughtily. Completely different to the way other inhabitants of Iran walk. My mother had Kurdish origins and, despite her small frame, she plied through the air like a colossus.

I open the package, assailed once again by *shanbelileh*. Inside I find my Babyliss, put back together and all in order. I rush to the bathroom and plug it in – it works. I go back to the package and find my photos, very nicely touched up and actually rather gorgeous. I look ten years younger. My eyebrows, which I never pluck, are prettily curved and my wrinkles smoothed away, as is the bump in my nose. I hope the official at the Ministry of the Interior will accept this non-identity photo.

I leaf absent-mindedly through their passports. They've clearly only been to Syria where Iranians go on a pilgrimage to the tomb of a sister of one of our Imams – I forget which. Before the Revolution no one went to Syria. But what with devaluation, visa problems and the Islamisation of the country, Syria has become the favourite destination for practising Muslims after Mecca – a compulsory pilgrimage for all Muslims – and the city of Karbala in Iraq – where the Imam Hosseyn, grandson of the Prophet, is laid to rest.

Before the Revolution the rich went to Switzerland, the not so rich to the United States and the lower middle class – the 'bazaar people', as they were known, like shoelace salesman – didn't travel. Nowadays charters to Syria are always full. My cleaning woman and her husband, Mohtaram and Hashem, have been there. When they came back all they could talk about was the king-size bed they'd slept in for the first time in their lives. They usually sleep in my apartment, in the workroom. As the only bed is reserved for the wife, the man sleeps on the bare floor. Honour is safe, at least under my roof.

A king-size bed so close to the sanctuary of a sister of a Shiite Imam . . . what an adventure!

I conscientiously fill out the photographers' forms, leaving blank the details of friends and relations in the country (they don't have any) as well as the names of their wives and children, which I don't know. I think I really should pay them: the favour I'm doing them (writing a few lines on a form) doesn't compare to the cost of photos and repairing a hairdryer. All the same, in my diary I strike out – definitively this time – the notes *Get passport photos* and *Repair hairdryer*.

Mission accomplished. I'm delighted to have completed two difficult tasks in the same day. When I call my friends to share my exploits with them, they all advise me to pay the photographers as soon as possible.

I put on the DVD *Rapunzel*, dubbed in Persian, for my three-year-old daughter Kiara, and we fall asleep on the sofa in the library.

Sunday

I wake up to the indisputable fact that I must confront the photographers again. The war of the *tarofs* will be waged: insistence that I pay on my part, stubborn refusal on theirs. I even think of a way round it – sending Mr Eskandari to their shop with the sum I owe them (or thereabouts), the half-filled-in forms and a letter of recommendation, so that once they're in Sweden they do everything they can to find our caretaker's missing son.

Yes, it's a good idea. I call my friend Nargess who is my main adviser in Iran, and ask her how much ID photos cost. She names a sum which strikes me as much lower than the usual price, but then she tends to undervalue everything. When she's shopping she always feels she's being swindled and the salesman hardly need say anything before she starts barking.

'How much is this vase?' she would ask in an bric-a-brac shop, for example.

'Forty thousand *tomans*.'

'What? What's going on?' she starts wailing. 'Do you think we're stupid, or something? Tell me, didn't your brother' – she's another one who's been using the informal you on everyone since the Revolution – 'buy this same vase from my mother for ten thousand *tomans*?'

'Yes, but that was ten years ago. At the time the dollar was at five hundred *tomans*,' the salesman usually replies, and he does have a point.

'Exactly, and now it's at a thousand *tomans*. So your vase shouldn't be worth more than twenty thousand!' proclaims Nargess, raising her voice, occasionally becoming so loud she's embarrassing.

At times like that I sometimes picture myself on Wall Street (again!) worrying about the rate of the dollar. Would a sudden and completely unexpected drop in the American currency tip the price of the vase in my favour?

One time a customer who'd stopped to watch one of our confabulations suddenly announced, 'I've seen the rate for the dollar today. It's at nine hundred and forty-five *tomans*.'

I forgot about the thing we were planning to buy and asked, 'And the euro?'

'One thousand one hundred and something.'

Apparently convinced that, on that particular day, her life depended on the rate of the euro, Nargess started thundering, 'No, no, it's at one thousand and ninety, not a *toman* more!'

She's like that. She argues about everything and will fight tooth and nail for her own interests and those of her friends. When I ask about the price of ID pictures on the phone she's very quick with her advice:

'Four thousand! And not a *toman* more!'

I thank her but decide to get a second opinion. I call my aunt, my mother's sister. In order to get her on the phone you inevitably have to go through two or three servants who constitute Mohtaram's and Hashem's entire lineage. Every time, even if I have seen them the day before, I have to ask for news not only of themselves but also of their children, their grandchildren and, since last year, their great-grandchildren.

'Hello, greetings to Samira, greetings to Somayeh, greetings to Sima, Mojdeh, Hamid and Vali, greetings to Kurosh, Monir, Kazem and Taleb . . . By the way, is my aunt there?'

The latter eventually takes the phone and gives a long sigh (if, by any chance, she isn't sighing then she's crying) because of her husband, my uncle, who has lost the use of his legs. I get straight down to asking her the price of ID photos.

'Well I don't know, how do you expect *me* to know?' she grumbles. 'Ask Nargess!'

While I'm telling her I've already asked Nargess I can hear her talking to Hamid, Mohtaram and Hashem's eldest son who works as her handyman and is probably just passing.

'Put the parcel down on the work surface!' she cries. 'No, no, not there, further along, further along!'

I'm just about to hang up when I hear my aunt say, 'Dr Bashiri's coming over later. I'll ask him about the photos.'

Dr Bashiri is the physiotherapist who goes to their house every day to reanimate my uncle's now inactive muscles. Along with his portable stretching equipment, he brings them all the news from about town. He's the official doctor for the national wrestling team and his youthfulness (he's twenty-eight) is a source of pride to my aunt. She can't mention him without pointing out the fact that, when the Shah left, he was only a year old.

Chubby Dr Bashiri also specialises in treating unwanted

body hair. Another source of pride for my aunt is telling
people he succeeded in removing ninety per cent of his
own wife's excess hair in less than a month. Dr Bashiri's
merits, so highly praised by my aunt, have spread all the
way to Washington where one of our exiled compatriots,
having fruitlessly sent her rather hairy daughter to one of
America's most renowned laser clinics, decided to entrust
her progeny to the young doctor.

This is the man supposed to inform me authoritatively
about the price of ID photos. He's apparently qualified to.
Why? I have no idea. I don't even ask.

I wait a couple of hours and the phone rings. It's
Hamid, my aunt's factotum.

'Hello, madam, are you well?' he begins.

'Yes, and you?'

'Thank you. And sir, is he well?'

'Thank you.'

'Kiara *djoun*, the beloved Kiara, is she well?'

'Thank you, she's very well.'

'My greetings to everyone.'

Now it's my turn to send greetings to his family:

'Hamid *djan*, dear Hamid, greetings to your wife, your
sons, your daughter, your sister and her daughters, greetings to your brothers and their children.'

'I will tell them how great and honourable you are. Dr
Bashiri would like to speak to you.'

First Dr Bashiri wants to know the price suggested by
Nargess. He obviously doesn't have a clue, and I feel I've
wasted a whole morning waiting for information from an
entrepreneurial doctor who, instead of informing, starts by
interrogating me. Sensing my reticence, he adds, 'I had
some ID photos done last year, when I accompanied our
wrestling team to Bahrain. Have you ever been to Bahrain?'

Before the conversation launches into an endless discussion of the sultanate of Bahrain and the remarkable progress that's been made there in two decades when we, in Iran, have only regressed . . . I give in: 'Four thousand *tomans*. Nargess said four thousand.'

'Yes, that's what I thought too. Round about four thousand. I paid less than three thousand last year. But with the dollar going up and up, and inflation . . .'

I take the opportunity to ask him the euro rate, out of habit, it's a reflex, because everyone automatically keeps thinking about it. Even Hamid, who's never set foot outside Iran.

'One thousand one hundred and fourteen *tomans* today.' I thank him.

'By the way, Nahal *khanoum*, Mrs Nahal,' he ventures before hanging up, 'would you be able to put me in touch with Adidas?'

'With Adidas?'

'Yes, I'll tell you why: I'd like to buy the rights for their brand for Iran. And if you'd be interested, we could even go into partnership.'

I can hear my aunt's voice behind him as she listens to the conversation, already celebrating free trainers and sneakers.

Without showing too much surprise, I politely decline Dr Bashiri's offer and make it clear that I don't really know anyone in sportswear in France. He presses the point, referring again to our possible partnership. I refuse even more politely, guessing that his proposal rests on the simple fact that I speak French. Dr Bashiri speaks English but an English learned in Iranian school after Persian and Arabic, or picked up on the internet and tested out as far as that's possible on foreign TV channels. He is one of those people who watch the news on CNN and the BBC (broadcast in English, of course), but are quite incapable of formulating the tiniest scrap of a sentence themselves except for 'good morning' and 'how are you'.

Still very politely, I stand my ground while trying not to humiliate the doctor for his linguistic failings, and I promise to try and find him a bilingual or even trilingual partner. I think of Nargess, who has already worked in the States for Benetton.

'No, no,' he interrupts me. 'This is a confidential offer, it could be very lucrative and might awaken the interest of the authorities. Discretion is essential.' Then he lowers his voice to add, 'I'll give you more details later.'

He doesn't want to talk about it on the phone. He probably suspects he's being tapped.

'Yes,' I say. 'OK, OK, we'll talk about it, definitely.'

Finally, I hang up. A whole morning wasted.

The videophone rings. Again that horizontal bar of the caretaker Mr Eskandari's moustache, and his voice telling me the two photographers are there. I don't want them to come up. I get ready to go down myself to pay them and give back the forms but an ancestral, primeval, ancient voice, a voice that sometimes speaks to me although I don't know where it's coming from, suggests I should invite them up. That's what people do, it's the custom. Part of me has absolutely no desire to ask them in, offer them tea, and embark on a conversation about how difficult it is for Iranians to integrate in foreign countries; another part of me knows that I can't do anything else. The voice (*my* voice) dictates it.

I press the button on the videophone.

'Send them up,' I tell the caretaker.

In the meantime I go into the bathroom, touch up my

lipstick and realise I'm wearing my Pleats outfit again. To Iranian eyes, the crinkled effect of the garment clearly betrays inborn flippancy. Quite impossible for them to imagine clothes could be created creased.

Never mind: I don't have time to change. They ring at the door. I call out to say it's open . . . it's always open.

As soon as they are inside the two men want to take off their shoes. Since the Revolution people have got into the habit of removing footwear the minute they're in an apartment. This too can be explained: the floor of premises where prayers are celebrated must not be trodden by dirty shoes. So every time I want to go to some government organisation (to the Ministry of Justice, for example, where they handle disputes arising from expropriations – of which my mother was a victim – in the first few years after the Revolution), I know I ought to take my shoes off before I approach the judge or the ministerial adviser, a be-turbaned religious figure. That means being sure to wear opaque socks that day so the red varnish on my toenails doesn't leap out at the judge, invalidating any request.

I still remember a scene two or three years ago when I addressed the entire male population of a village in the north. The gathering was composed of men who had made the most of the Revolution to seize my mother's land. As I stood before them with no shoes, which was as it should be, all I could think of was hiding my nail varnish: I curled one foot over the other, careful to cover it up.

I decide to let the photographers come in in their footwear. Just the thought of them taking off their tired old shoes with their backs flattened down (in memory of age-old *babouches* which didn't have backs), and putting them by the door to my apartment at the feet of a standing

Buddha where I keep Japanese incense burning the whole time . . . well, it makes me feel a bit sick. I'd rather they kept them on. I insist, even. I slip four thousand *tomans* into an envelope, and the two men come into my sitting room with their shoes still on their feet.

Mohtaram, the cleaner who was already working for us in my mother's day, brings us tea. As a young woman Mohtaram had bronzed skin, a thin, almost bony nose and a svelte figure. All she longed for, though, were white skin, a fleshy nose and a curvaceous body. My mother and I used to think that, had she been born into a wealthier family, her wickedly fashionable physique would have helped her marry a banker's son and spend her holidays in Gstaad instead of Qom. In the end, a bit plumper but still tanned, she came to live in my apartment and do whatever I needed on my trips to Iran. Her hair is hidden beneath a scarf, like in the old days under the Shah's regime, but what has changed since then is that she no longer wears a chador. Like all other non-chador women, when she goes out Mohtaram puts on a simple coat which hides her figure.

The fact that I have a cleaner, which proves I'm from a good family, puts an end to the photographers' informal style of address once and for all. I thank them for the hairdryer, and hand them the forms and the envelope. They take the documents but put the envelope down on the coffee table without opening it.

The *tarof* begins. No, they don't want any payment. It's out of the question. This goes on for a good half-hour during which, knowing I will eventually give in, I try to think how else I can remunerate them. During the conversation I gather that their wives, who also work together, are seamstresses. I think I'm saved. I actually have the last few issues of *Vogue*, smuggled back from a trip to Paris – at the risk of being arrested by customs officers. Yes, in customs they really do ask every woman coming into Iran whether she is carrying any videos or *burda*. In their vocabulary, the word *burda* is a generic term for fashion magazines. Copies confiscated like this are sent to the Ministry for Islamic Guidance, into the hands of a conscientious employee who spends all day colouring in by hand the models' naked hands, legs and arms so that they conform to the official image of an Islamic woman.

The Colouring Office is also responsible for blackening museum brochures and art books. It's an all-embracing make-up operation. At a time when, on the website avizoon.com, young Iranian women from modest backgrounds – you can tell that at a glance from the rustic simplicity of the furniture behind them – exhibit their genitalia for all the world to see, a civil servant with a black marker pen carefully blots out Aphrodite's breasts in the catalogue for the Louvre.

I'm sure that my – uncoloured – copies of *Vogue* will fully satisfy my visitors, and certainly their wives. But when I try to offer them to them I can feel terrible disapproval from Mohtaram, who's serving us a second cup of tea. As far as she's concerned, anything in my apartment is mine and anything that leaves it is hers. When an iron stops working there's no question of having it repaired. I have to give it to Mohtaram. That's the rule and it's all the more strict for being unformulated. In light of this, the repair of the hairdryer represented a veritable betrayal on my part, an affirmation that these everyday things were still my property even outside my home, which is literally inconceivable.

Mohtaram throws nothing away. Absolutely nothing.

She fishes out my empty shampoo bottles, fills them with soapy mousse and displays them, like ornaments, on the basin in her own apartment.

Predicting (and her instinct is right) that the three issues of *Vogue* are going to escape her clutches, she slopes bitterly back to the kitchen and doesn't answer the phone which is ringing. With the three magazines in my hand, I quickly calculate that the price of one copy, if it's possible to put a figure on it, is higher than the cost of the ID photos, and that giving away all three, besides the risk of seriously upsetting Mohtaram, might appear provocative, arrogant and almost suspect in its generosity. Without pausing or thinking, I hand them two issues and, with a wide smile, say, 'A copy of *Vogue* for each of your wives.'

Mohtaram, who's listening from the kitchen, then agrees to pick up the phone, which is still ringing. She knows she's just salvaged the third copy which can now grace her coffee table – and that too came from me, last year when I rearranged my apartment.

Mohtaram tells me Nargess is on the phone for me. I go into the kitchen and tell my friend, who wants to know whether the four thousand *tomans* satisfied the photographers, that I've settled the matter by giving them two recent issues of *Vogue*.

'Two issues of *Vogue*!' she protests vehemently.

Even Mohtaram, who catches her reaction, nods in agreement with my friend's annoyance.

'You wait!' Nargess goes on. 'They'll sell your magazines in their studio for ten times the price of your photos!'

'They're not going to sell them. I offered them to their wives who are seamstresses.'

'Seamstresses? Their wives are seamstresses?'

'Yes, that's what they said. They work together.'

Nargess's voice has just changed. I can tell she's thinking. A moment later she's off again. 'Do you know what you could do? Show them the chairs you want re-covering.'

'Do you think so?'

'Of course. Show them the chairs.'

In fact there's only one thing I want: for them to leave as soon as possible with their magazines. I go back to the sitting room and there, in spite of myself, I can't help a quick peek at the chairs: they are covered in fabric which, in my opinion, doesn't go with the rest of the furniture. I've already asked several upholsterers to come and take them away to re-cover them, but they all refused for a variety of reasons.

'Do your wives also work in interior design?' I ask my visitors.

'What sort of thing?'

Without waiting a moment longer, I show them the chairs.

'Do they do furnishings? These chairs, for example, would they be able to re-cover them?'

They examine them carefully and catch each other's eye.

'Of course. No problem,' announces Morad.

And they agree to take them away there and then. I nip out to find the fabric, which I've already bought – some simple jute. I go back into the sitting room and hand them the roll.

They can't get over it: covering French eighteenth-century-style chairs (the height of refinement in their eyes) in a coarse shapeless fabric? Yet again I insist. I'm used to this sort of reaction; when a few years ago, after my mother died, I sold her Gustavian furniture bought in Sweden in the 1970s and replaced it with wrought-iron tables and

consoles . . . well, with the exception of the designer and
myself, only three or four people approved of my choice,
and one of them was Nargess, who admires modern interior design while not accepting the cost of it.

The photographer-hairdryer repairers try politely to dissuade me. They struggle to convince me that these chairs
warrant more classy fabric worthy of me and my apartment. But all their efforts are in vain. That really is the
fabric I want.

Nargess rings back. She's been thinking. This time she
advises me not to give them the whole piece of cloth.

'Why?' I ask quietly.

'They'll never give you back the offcuts.'

I take the risk. I have no desire to watch them, here, in
my apartment, scissors in hand, unrolling the fabric and
setting about cutting it up. Let them take the whole roll.
Who cares?

'And another thing,' Nargess goes on. 'I've done some
research. For your new passport you don't have to go the
Central Passport Office. There's an office in every district
to do that now. I've just been past my local one, it's full to
bursting. People sleep outside the building all night to get
in first thing in the morning.'

I tell her I'll go and check for myself, reckoning there's
no good reason why passport offices should suddenly be in
pandemonium.

'But they're in the process of computerising the whole
system!' she replies. 'Didn't you know? Last year it took
two days to renew a passport. Now it takes a month!'

That 'they', that third person plural denotes the current
Islamic administration. That 'they' is a way of saying it's
not 'us'.

'Are you sure of that?'

'Absolutely certain.'

'And what if I don't want to spend the night on the street?'

'They suggest – in fact they encourage – people to send the documents by post. But then it takes even longer. Two or three months.'

'Well, what am I going to do?'

My husband, who's French, is getting impatient, I can hear it in his voice when he calls from Paris. My thirty days of anticipated absence are almost up. I have to get back.

'Nargess, there's no way I can wait a month for a new passport. Are you really sure about this?'

'Go and see for yourself! People spend the whole night there! Everyone shouts but it doesn't do them any good. Go and see if you don't believe me!'

Spending the night waiting isn't actually a problem. I can send one of Mohtaram's sons to queue for me. But how can I wait here another month without my husband getting angry? How can I explain to him that – in Tehran, in this day and age, for obscure reasons connected with computerisation – renewing a passport can take more than a month?

I ask Nargess whether she happens to know anyone at the Central Passport Office. After a pause she suggests I ask Dr Bashiri, my uncle's physio.

I don't want to go through Dr Bashiri, or Adidas shoes, the sultanate of Bahrain and all that . . . No!

'Can you think of anyone else?'

'I'll ask my boss's bodyguards. They're in the secret service,' says Nargess. 'They might have an idea.'

I hang up feeling helpless, and go back into the sitting room. The photographers, who have heard everything, then inform me (still utterly politely and kindly) that they know a doctor who would probably be in a position to sort out my passport problem.

A doctor? Why a doctor? Not giving a direct answer, Morad wants to know whether there would be any problem if the doctor in question called me this evening, even rather late. I give him my landline and mobile numbers. Odd, in less than twenty-four hours Hassan *agha* and *agha* Morad (Mr Hassan and Mr Morad) have become indispensable to me.

Hassan eventually goes over to the coffee table and picks up the forms. We shake hands, a gesture outlawed by the Revolution: since the Islamic Republic was instated it has been strictly forbidden and seen as contemptible because touching a woman's hand could arouse a man, making him completely lose control and leading away from the path of righteousness. Since the Revolution, the Islamic male has become particularly vulnerable and threatened . . . I often wonder why.

Like all Iranian women, I took a long time learning not to shake men's hands. Like them, I initially confined this ban to men in the outside world, in administrative roles, at universities or hospitals. But it was not long before doubts crept in. In a family gathering, for example, should I shake hands with strangers invited by my parents? One childhood friend descended from the Qadjars – the royal dynasty before the Pahlavis – suddenly became a strict Muslim and stopped shaking women by the hand. I wasn't up to speed on this transformation and when I bumped into him at my aunt's house and started towards him with open arms to kiss him as I always had, he hastily backed away. At the time I thought that, having married a practising Muslim, he wanted to avoid kissing any other woman but when I held out my hand to him he backed away even further as if in panic.

And there's more. The new Islam forbids not only *contact* with a stranger, a *na mahram*, a man who is not part of the immediate family – father, brother or son – but also forbids looking him in the eye.

I was used to smiling at any man, shaking his hand, possibly even kissing him on the cheek and looking him in the eye but then, like all other women and absolutely overnight, I had to restrain myself: no smiling, no proffering a hand or a cheek and (hardest of all) no looking at the person I was talking to. Learning to look away – who'd have thought!

Thirty years of Islamic law have still not succeeded in completely wiping out these 'perverse acts'. I gather that the ban on hand-shaking has recently been withdrawn for Iranian diplomats. France and Iran almost broke off relations following an incident when Mrs Chirac proffered her hand and the Iranian ambassador refused to shake it. The matter had to be cleared up by the Guide himself, Ayatollah Khameneyi who – through gritted teeth – permitted this exception. Even now, all these years on, I can get so hopelessly confused that I refuse to shake hands with a cousin, or cheerfully embrace a perfect stranger, or greet very close friends by joining my hands in front of my face like an Indian woman.

The two photographers leave with my twelve chairs and a whole roll of jute. I'm satisfied. I have my identity photos, my hairdryer is repaired, my chairs have been taken away (it took several trips) and Morad and Hassan have promised that the doctor they know will get me out of queuing overnight at the local passport office.

I go into the library, which I have left untouched out of respect for my parents' books, given that they were both writers. Looking at their books, those they read and those they wrote, is to look at my parents themselves, as if they were still here.

My daughter, who goes to my aunt during the day, has left toys scattered about and I'm just clearing them away when Mohtaram appears in the room with the two issues of *Vogue*. The photographers have deliberately forgotten the magazines, pushing the *tarof* to extremes.

I fly out to the terrace. They are just crossing the street.

'You've forgotten the copies of *Vogue*!' I cry.

They know what I mean but still ask, 'The what?'

'The copies of *Vogue*!' I say, brandishing them. Then I throw them down. The wind carries them in a tumbling fall which, for a brief moment, contaminates the purified air of Islamic Iran with images of miniskirts and hot pants. Mr Eskandari deftly takes delivery of them at the foot of the building. He looks up at me, his eyes shining in the hope of finally having some news from Sweden thanks to these travellers-to-be who will surely follow up leads on his ghost son. In surety, or as a deposit, he triumphantly hands them the two copies of *Vogue*.

They wave and walk away, each carrying four chairs. The rest are waiting by the door under Mr Eskandari's watchful eye. The photographers will be back to make further trips.

I spend the evening at my aunt's house, surrounded by her retinue of servants, all more idle than each other. Three people live and work in her home without affording her the least comfort. She cleans, irons and cooks for herself, watched indulgently by Hamid, his wife Masserat and sister Samira. They are Mohtaram's son, daughter-in-law and daughter respectively.

My aunt is one of the most adorable women I know. A very long time ago her husband, who was about forty at the time, decided to stop working and live off his private income. Besotted by his green eyes – when ninety-nine per cent of Iranians have dark brown eyes – my aunt made no protest and settled for an income which shrank a little every year. When she compares her life now to that of some of her friends, who have become very wealthy, my aunt never fails to remind them that, in the days when their husbands got about in second-hand cars, her handsome green-eyed provider owned the only white Thunderbird in the capital, a vehicle even the Shah coveted. Now all she has is a small apartment in an ageing block in Tehran, but whenever her friend Jaleh is mentioned – and this a woman who lives between Antibes, Gstaad and Aspen – she can't help reminding us she lent her wedding dress, a designer gown, to the selfsame Jaleh to help launch her in married life.

I ring the bell and Masserat opens the door to me. I kiss her and then Samira. Masserat is a fat woman of about thirty who, with my aunt's encouragement, is following a weight-loss diet from a Swedish medical magazine. The technique is simple, the author tells whoever will listen: 'To start with, halve the amount of food you usually eat for about ten days, then halve it again for another ten days, and so on.' I'm not sure what stage of reductions Masserat has currently reached but, judging by the spare tyres bulging beneath the orange-sequined T-shirt I gave her, she hasn't yet passed the decisive milestone of the first ten days.

Samira, her sister-in-law, is already a grandmother at forty, and her granddaughter has the same name as me – which is why Mohtaram nicknames her *khanoum* (Mrs) out of respect for me. Samira is a pretty woman but for the absence, for want of proper care, of any front teeth. Another instance where my bank account, accessed by my aunt's power of attorney, came into play, contributing to the installation of a row of false teeth at a favourable rate, thanks to a dentist who was a long-standing friend.

Then I shake Hamid's hand. The fact that he holds his hand out to me is as good a way as any of resisting the Islamic regime. He prays, he fasts, he makes his wife wear the veil . . . but he shakes my hand. In all its triumphant progress the Revolution forgot Hamid and people like him – in other words, most of Iran.

My aunt takes me to see my uncle whose bed has pride of place in the living room. My uncle, as I've said, can no longer walk. Before he lost the use of his legs, he gave up venturing out of town, then his neighbourhood, then his house. After breakfast and again after lunch he would take a couple of cushions and settle himself comfortably on the sofa, where he stayed for the rest of the day. Come the evening he'd get up to sit at the table, then he'd go to bed for the night. I see his paralysis as a reprisal from nature: 'You don't want us,' his legs seem to be saying. 'Well, goodbye then, we're giving up on you.'

They don't have any children. All her life my aunt has regretted failing to perpetuate the rare genes of her green-eyed man. When they married she gave him her inheritance, the proceeds of selling hundreds of hectares of land in northern Iran, and she has always agreed with his every decision, just for the green of his eyes. Gradually, over the years, she has made him her child. She has even found herself delighting in his having an extramarital affair. At least it means he's having fun, she said.

My uncle doesn't speak, or speaks very little. When he does say something it's usually to attack or even insult the person he's talking to. Their friends only see them for my aunt's gentleness and good nature. Yet, in her boundless love for her husband, she claims the exact opposite: 'So-and-so only comes if you're here, you know. The man at the pâtisserie has made a cake specially for you, just the way you like it, and the butcher's saving his best cut, from the fillet, which you love.'

None of this is true. I've never known whether my uncle really believes her. Does he genuinely think my aunt's closest friends only agree to visit if he himself is at home, or the pastry chef kneads the dough for him alone, or the butcher — forgetting all his beautiful women customers — seeks out hidden treasures in his cold room on his account?

Hamid, Mohtaram's son, is forty-two. Before my aunt took him on as a general handyman to look after her invalid husband, he and his wife and three children lived in a basement rented out of his wife's salary — she worked as a childminder for a cousin. Like the majority of young Iranians, Hamid took opium. My aunt employed him for the simple reason that she couldn't have a stranger in the house overnight, and chose to ignore her new gofer's yellowed face, hollow cheeks, ruined teeth and limp demeanour.

She hoped that, pampered by her, Hamid would detoxify pretty quickly. In vain. All the same, thanks to a salary well above the usual remuneration, he moved into a ground-floor flat (the first sign of rising up the social ladder), bought a bed for his eldest daughter who had ambitions of going to university, and eventually bought himself a mobile phone. When he first started working for my aunt, when the poor woman's tears flowed from morning till night and a succession of doctors trooped to my uncle's bedside, Hamid took me to one side and asked quietly whether he could borrow my mobile.

I explained that it hadn't worked since my daughter threw it down the loo.

'It doesn't matter if it's not working,' he replied. 'I just want to put it in the back pocket of my jeans.'

'The back pocket of your jeans?' I repeated in amazement.

While this was going on, the highly reputable surgeon who was visiting that day frantically interrogated every member of Mohtaram's family in an attempt to find a television so he could watch Bush making an announcement on CNN about Iran's nuclear capabilities.

Unperturbed, Hamid turned round and slipped his hand into his back pocket.

'You see,' he said. 'I want the mobile to stick out of my pocket. Like this. I want it to be visible.'

I left him for a moment and showed the surgeon which room the television was in. While I was there I took the drowned mobile from my handbag and gave it to Hamid, who slipped it straight into his back pocket.

The phone roamed around my aunt's apartment like that for several months under the noses of the capital's most eminently qualified medical experts.

Nowadays he has a real mobile peeping out of his jeans pocket. No more pretence. Sometimes the thing even rings.

Hamid brings in a tray for me with a cup of coffee and a glass of low-alcohol beer. The latter, along with other forbidden drinks, is delivered to my aunt's apartment on request by an Armenian acquaintance.

Hamid knows that when I come to see my aunt during the day I ask for coffee not, like every other guest, tea. He offers me the tray.

'A beer and a coffee,' he says.

This coffee, which I haven't said I want, means Hamid is planning to ask me for something – a job for his brother or a statement saying he has finished his military service (when he's actually a deserter). It can't be to do with money because when Hamid is short my aunt is the one who takes care of the situation, abusing her power of attorney over my bank account before I've even given my consent. It was only well into the process that I discovered I was financing the education of one of Mohtaram's grand-daughters in this way.

I pour myself some beer. Hamid stays in the living room, tray in hand. I'm sitting on the edge of my uncle's bed, encouraging him to drink. Hamid still doesn't move. Here we go, he's going to ask me for the end of military service statement, I think to myself.

Just then my aunt comes out of the kitchen, briefly abandoning Masserat and Samira, her favoured sources of conversation – she chats to them all day long while she gets on with their work. She comes over to me and announces that, according to Dr Bashiri, the laptop one of my friends gave them is completely obsolete and might as well be chucked out. Hamid nods, but I don't agree. When he gave it to my aunt, my friend just recommended having it overhauled. From that to throwing it out

I'm suddenly struck by the comparison between Mohtaram's pride in exhibiting my shampoo bottles and Hamid's expression as he tries to encourage me to throw away a Toshiba laptop fresh from England. I smell a plot. Definitely. My aunt is clearly in cahoots with Hamid. Since my uncle has been paralysed she's been haunted by one thought: Hamid leaving. So she anticipates his every desire. Before the heat even begins to melt the tarmac on the streets of Tehran – and perhaps some day all its inhabitants – my aunt thinks of giving Hamid electric fans. Even cousins coming back from trips to the States compete to please my aunt, pitching in with Calvin Klein shirts and Ralph Lauren polo shirts.

Thin, wan and utterly useless, Hamid divides his time between his silence and opening his presents.

Dr Bashiri's diagnosis about the state of the laptop must be a strategy of my aunt's to try and justify her generosity to Hamid, giving him a computer that has been pronounced worthless. Still, I'm resisting my aunt's efforts and Hamid's cup of coffee. I tell them I'll go to the computer centre at Paytakht to have the laptop overhauled myself. But I immediately repent. How would I get there? Paytakht is on the outskirts of the area where traffic is limited, but the recent scheme allowing cars with odd and even registration numbers to travel on alternate days has reduced trips even further.

And who would I go with? Why lose a morning, or more, having a laptop repaired when my aunt will probably never use it and will, anyway, end up giving it to Hamid?

I dig my heels in. I will go to Paytakht, come what may. Bad luck.

Hamid goes back to the kitchen with the tray of coffee. I know he won't bring the beer again.

My phone rings.

'I'm Dr Askarnia,' announces a voice. '*Agha* Morad gave me your number. What can I do for you?'

I explain that I need to get back to France urgently for a conference and my passport is out of date, that I didn't realise how the new system worked, and that I can't queue all night outside the local passport office or wait a whole month.

'*Agha* Morad and Hassan *agha* are my brothers,' he replied. 'I would do anything for them.'

Given that he began with a statement about their family relationship, I know immediately I will have to pay, even very dearly. I daren't ask him how much it will cost. That's just not done. He would hang up on me even if he were banking on asking me for money – which he almost certainly is.

'Be at the front door of the Central Passport Office in Shahrara at nine o'clock tomorrow morning,' Dr Askarnia tells me.

'But passport renewals are only done in local offices now . . .' I say.

'I know, I know. But the officer I know works at Shahrara. That's where we need to go. You'll recognise me straight away. I look like Dâryoush.'

Dâryoush but not so tall, he clarifies.

Phew. This reference to Dâryoush – the 1970s singer and superstar, my childhood idol – means Dr Askarnia isn't one of 'them'. Otherwise he wouldn't have mentioned Dâryoush. I deduce that, if I do meet him tomorrow, I will probably feel perfectly comfortable with him.

I thank him and assure him I will be there at nine o'clock.

I go to find my aunt in the kitchen to announce proudly that I have succeeded, under my own steam, in avoiding the unavoidable queues for renewing a passport. Still, a little voice inside me – my little voice, the one that has acted as my mother's voice since she died – warns me of the risks I'm running. Entrusting my passport to a doctor who looks like a singer, a man recommended by two photographers from the Ecbatana studio whom I've known barely twenty-four hours, is far from constituting a guarantee of success. But my pride in feeling independent, and in escaping my aunt's contacts and kindly meant machinations, make me ignore the little voice.

'I'll go to Shahrara tomorrow and then on to Paytakht.'

My aunt usually tells her husband everything. When they came home from supper in town in the days when my uncle could still walk, she would describe in detail the evening they had only just finished. She covered everything: the names of the guests, the dresses and shoes, how the menu was put together . . . She always lives everything twice. Even before she was married, when she came home from the cinema with her best friend, she would tell her the story of the film they had just seen.

Despite my uncle's sleepy state, she rushes over to let him know how audacious I have been. Since he has been paralysed, my uncle has opted for a general vacancy of all his senses. His voice quavers, his green eyes are unfocused, his ears don't seem to hear anything. Yet, when he is told my story, he sits up slightly, starts coughing gently and eventually announces in a firm voice that he wants to challenge my decision.

My uncle is afraid of everything. He has always been afraid, all his life. Despite his unparalleled honesty – probably due to more than forty years' inactivity – he used to be frightened of the Savak, the Shah's secret service, rather as he now fears the same force of the Islamic Republic. Every passport renewal translated itself into a week of insomnia and hours spent in my aunt's arms as she comforted him and patiently explained there was no threat to him, none at all. When a lack of time forced him to go to the Central Passport Office – the place I myself have to go to at nine o'clock tomorrow to meet the spitting image, in reduced form, of Dâryoush – he would make sure a cousin or friend went with him. They would be quite useless, of course, but he paid them for the trip.

So renewing a passport is a serious matter for my uncle, almost a tragedy, requiring powerful sleeping pills, an understanding partner, and friends with time to spare. The thought that I'm going to undertake this battle without meeting all these conditions is inconceivable to him. After a long irrelevant preamble about how the English will never leave Iran alone, he demonstrates his utter disapproval of what I'm planning. My aunt nods in agreement as he speaks.

The chapter on England is because my uncle is from that generation of Iranians who see the secret hand of English intervention in everything – not only in Iran and the Middle East but also in Europe and the United States. The English are everywhere. They're ruling the world. According to my uncle, the US President is a mere puppet in the British Prime Minister's hands, never making any decision without consulting him. The Knesset acts on orders from the House of Lords, as do the Lebanese Hezbollah and Iranian ayatollahs. There's no point asking him, 'In that case, why are they at war with each other?' He gets angry and replies tartly, 'I speak in Persian, don't I?'

Rejecting Britain's possible stranglehold on Iran's Central Passport Office (which strikes me as improbable), I tell my uncle yet again that I need my passport.

'I'm against it,' he interrupts me. 'I speak in Persian, don't I?'

His hands start shaking again, his body goes limp and he slumps down. He resumes his paralysed position. I know the discussion is closed.

To neutralise the persistent warnings from my little voice, I really do need approval from somewhere. I won't find it in my aunt: she never contradicts her husband. It's already late but I know I can call Nargess. Which I do. She is in her car: she has just been to a bookshop to pick up some books ordered by a close friend in Paris, and is now taking them to an air hostess flying to France tomorrow. I act as a mouthpiece for my little voice and briefly explain my concerns: I'm suddenly surrounded by strangers carrying away my chairs, arranging to meet me out on the street the next day . . .

In amongst the insults she hurls at passers-by and other road users, Nargess gives me the thumbs-up: 'You've got nothing to worry about . . . Son of a bitch, slow down! Let me through! While you're there you should also ask this doctor if he can get you a national ID card.'

I immediately reject the idea of getting my hands on an ID card, the much-publicised *kart-e melli*. According to Dr Bashiri, Hamid and my aunt, the very first step – which consists of going to the Central Bank to pay for registering this *kart-e melli* – means queuing for six or seven hours. '*Kart-e melli, badan, badan*,' another time, another time, I think to myself, thereby scorning the acquisition of this document without which no legal undertaking is possible. No, I won't be asking Dâryoush for a *kart-e melli*. It's my passport I want.

'One last thing . . .' I say to Nargess.

She has reached the air hostess's flat. I can hear her saying hello.

'What?' she picks me up again.

'How much should I give him?'

'Nothing! You give him absolutely nothing! When he gives you your new passport, check with the photographers. For now, nothing!'

I can hear her explaining to the air hostess and the girl's husband that a Dâryoush look-alike, only shorter, has offered to arrange my passport renewal. I want to hang up as soon as possible because I'm worried about their reaction, and perhaps even their mocking laughter.

I say goodbye. Nargess's last word is very firm: 'Nothing, do you hear me? Don't give him anything!'

A little later someone rings the doorbell. It's a young cousin. She has brought back my daughter, whom she took to an amusement park for the evening with her son. It all went very well, apparently.

I feel exhausted. Hamid, who has hung on to his brother's car, drives us home with Kiara already asleep.

Monday

The morning alarm is immediately followed by my checking all my documents: Islamic photographs, identity card (soon to be obsolete) and the number of my future *kart-e melli*, miraculously obtained on the telephone simply by giving my date of birth. I dress in an Islamically correct way: wide trousers, long coat and oversize scarf. I put a discreet touch of make-up on – some barely visible lipstick intended for my own satisfaction – and call for an *ajans*, a taxi.

As I climb into the taxi I tell the driver where I'm going, 'The Central Passport Office in Shahrara, please.'

Working for an *ajans*, which means being a taxi driver, has become a second job for a good many city-dwelling Iranians. Without realising it, you can be driven around by a maths professor whose salary barely reaches the equivalent of two hundred pounds a month while the rent on his one-bedroom flat far exceeds that sum. You could get a driver who has just arrived in the capital and speaks only Turkish, the language (although few people realise this) of more than a third of the Iranian population.

One time, coming home from a party, I even got into an *ajans* with an invisible driver. His head was barely higher than the steering wheel because he had pushed the seat so far back and put the backrest so low. The car smelt of hash. That was another time when my little voice intervened, trying to dissuade me from getting in. But I'd already opened the door and said hello to the – virtually horizontal – driver. Shyness, or courtesy, outstripped the little voice so I sat down in the car and quickly gave the address. The taxi set off to New Age music from an MP3 player on the dashboard, where a screen gave a visual interpretation of the sounds.

'Do you know anything about New Age?' the supine man asked me, making no attempt to disguise his apathy.

I noticed he wasn't using the informal address and, so as not to lose face, quickly answered, 'Do you have any Peter Gabriel?'

Prostrate as he was, I wondered how he could drive and started seriously regretting the triumph of my shyness over the little voice.

He reached out a hand, took the remote control for the audio-visual system from the passenger seat (his relaxed position making it impossible for him to reach the dashboard) and instantly put on a Peter Gabriel track. All the way home I wondered what the driver's other job could be: DJ in a clandestine nightclub, waiter in Monsoon, the local Buddha Bar?

My driver today sports a thick moustache and three days' worth of beard, which may mean he is observing the Islamic law which states that a man should not shave completely (I've never worked out why).

'You can't renew passports in Shahrara any more,' he warns me. 'It has to be done in local offices.'

'Yes, I know,' I say, not adding anything else. I'm afraid to get into conversation. If I do he might convince me not to see Dâryoush and could even suggest someone else's services. My aunt, who constantly bemoans her misfortunes to taxi drivers, rang me once to tell me she had just been in a taxi and the driver's cousin's neighbour was a bodyguard to the Supreme Guide and could talk to him about my long-standing petition – about our confiscated lands in Mazandaran, in the north, which I have been struggling to have restored for years – and that this man, the driver's cousin's neighbour, might be able to intervene in my favour.

So I add nothing else. When we arrive at Shahrara I tell him I'm hiring him for the whole morning. I get out and wait for Dâryoush's dead spit by the front door of the premises. People walk by but I don't pay them any attention. Not one of them looks like my idol. Perched on some piping from nearby building work, I catch myself singing Dâryoush's biggest hit.

I sing all the words – right to the end, happy to have temporarily stifled my little voice, the voice that is aware and conscious and has a mission to warn me of danger.

Dâryoush is obviously late. I call him on his mobile. He will be here in ten minutes, he reassures me. Half an hour passes and then I do indeed see the spitting image of Dâryoush getting out of a van: same full beard, same sparse eyebrows, same perfect nose, which is rare in an Iranian, same sad smile. Just smaller. But I was warned. I get up and say hello to him – without shaking his hand. He talks effusively, as if to an old friend, while he takes his briefcase from the back of his van.

'For now we need to get hold of the form,' he tells me. I look through the fence at the queue for the counter that hands out forms, and deduce that we have a good hour's wait. Not even glancing in that direction, Dâryoush asks me to follow him. We head towards the front door of a bank a little further along where a row of cars are parked under a sign saying NO PARKING. ALL VEHICLES WILL BE REMOVED.

Here two men are discreetly selling forms. Dâryoush, using his real name, Dr Askarnia, suggests I should buy one from them.

'Then we won't have to queue,' he explains.

I pay. The price, fifty times more than the legal rate, is justified by the fact that the two men also fill out the document. They know how to.

Dr Askarnia suggests I give them my passport. This time the little voice doesn't even have time to protest because I retort that I know how to fill in forms myself.

Dâryoush doesn't look convinced.

'They're used to it,' he insists. 'They can answer the questions professionally.'

I wonder about the amateur way of filling boxes marked 'Address' and 'Father's name' . . .

'And their writing's legible,' he adds, taking my passport.

I let myself be persuaded. One of them puts the form on the boot of a car and starts filling it in. Just in case, I keep an eye on what he's doing. When he gets to the box marked 'Employment', the man automatically puts 'Housewife'. I protest: I have a doctorate, I give conferences, I publish books!

'That's all we need – for him to put "writer"!' Dâryoush says sarcastically. 'Don't you see? Not only would it be impossible to rush through your application but you'd have to wait a long time, a very long time, before they even looked at your file! Think about it!'

He has a point. I'm beginning to realise that there really is a professional way to answer banal questions on a form. In the box marked 'Reason for travel' he puts 'Tourism'.

'That's wrong,' I whisper in Dâryoush's ear. 'It's for a conference I'm giving about the relationship between Buddhism and Iranian mysticism.'

Paying absolutely no attention to my comment, Dâryoush encourages the scribe, 'That's it, that's it, carry on.'

Then he suddenly looks up at me, stares for five or six seconds and announces baldly, 'You're magnesium deficient. You don't sleep well, do you?'

I do in fact have a magnesium deficiency but I sleep very well. Without taking my eyes off the form which is being filled out at great speed, I tell him I'm in good health.

'I'm a doctor,' he insists. 'It's perfectly clear that you're not.'

All at once, as if to prove him right, I feel my head spin and my blood pressure crash. For a moment I think perhaps I ought to admit that my blood pressure is very low and I frequently have dizzy spells.

But my little voice resists this confession. And it's right. I mustn't expose my weaknesses to this man. I don't say anything.

The form has been filled out. I'm an Iranian housewife going to Paris as a tourist. To rectify my drop in blood pressure I fish around in my handbag for a caramel. Problem: I've only got two. Including the two scribes, there are four of us, and before eating any kind of food it's customary to offer some to the company present. As I can't see myself cutting the sweets in half, I give up on my caramel, favouring giddiness over inevitably sticky fingers.

Dâryoush and I eventually bid farewell to the scribes and head back to the entrance gate. But all of a sudden, when we are only about three metres from the gateway, a man appears from nowhere and accosts Dâryoush.

'I came here today specially to see you!'

The man is about thirty, sporting a thick moustache. The collar of his shirt, which must at some time have been white, is buttoned up neatly. His trousers are too short but his shoes seem well polished.

My little voice points out that Dâryoush meets his 'clients' on the pavement outside the Central Passport office at about ten o'clock every day. Is that normal? Shouldn't I be a bit wary? I don't set any store by these warnings, though. Dâryoush goes over and shakes the man warmly by the hand. His name is Madjid, at least that's what Dâryoush calls him.

'Madjid *djan*, my dear Madjid,' he says. 'I didn't recognise you straight away. What's happened to you? You don't look so good.'

My little voice narrows things down a bit: Dâryoush doesn't see his clients but his patients outside the Central Passport Office at ten o'clock every day. This is where he does his consultations.

'Open your mouth, stick out your tongue.'

Madjid does as he is told. I try, in vain, to avoid looking at Madjid's teeth full of fillings and his fleshy tongue. After this very brief examination the patient grabs Dâryoush's hand.

'Doctor *djan*,' he cries, 'please help me, I beg you. It's not my health that's the problem. You're all I have. You're the only one who can help me.'

Dâryoush, alias Dr Askarnia, asks me to forgive him and says '*Force majeure*' in French with a strong Persian accent.

I sit back down on the piping and, in spite of myself, listen to their conversation. I don't know either of them but can't quite make up my mind to leave.

'Doctor *djan*, listen to me . . . I urgently need an eye.'

Dâryoush doesn't look in the least surprised.

'Have you got a pen and paper?' he asks straight away.

Madjid takes a worn notebook from the inside pocket of his jacket and hands it to him. Dâryoush scribbles a few words.

'You're going to go right now and see Dr Sahabi and say I sent you,' he says. 'Sahabi. Here's his address. I don't have his phone number. If his secretary won't let you in, tell her to call me. I'm putting my mobile number here. Can you read my writing?'

All the vigilance of my little voice is swept aside by this search for an eye. My reasoning has been called into play, it can't help wondering exactly who Dâryoush is. A real doctor? An organ trafficker? A charlatan simply trying to impress me with this performance with the sole aim of pumping up the price for the service he's providing for me?

I feel like calling Nargess, but resist the urge.

Madjid glances at Dâryoush's scribbling. He doesn't look convinced. Dâryoush points to Dr Sahabi's name on the notebook and explains more fully, 'Make sure you tell him the morgue will send him a new pair of eyes tomorrow morning, and he can give you one of the ones he has at his surgery. Make sure he knows that. Do you understand? He won't be short of eyes. Absolutely definitely. I'll guarantee it myself.'

I'm still sitting on the pipes from the building work. All I have to do is get up, walk round the two men, get into the *ajans* waiting for me on the other side of the street and go back to the sane world, the calm ordinary world, the one where you can't negotiate over pairs of eyes – complete with references to the morgue – outside the Central Passport Office. I don't move, though.

'You're sure he'll give me the eye, just like that, without a prescription?'

'Yes. But you must tell him you know me. Get him to call me if he's worried about anything,' he adds then turns to me and repeats the words '*force majeure*'.

I'm longing to know what Madjid wants to do with an eye. Dâryoush probably does too because in the end he asks, 'By the way, who do you want this eye for?'

'Doctor *djan*, a week ago I took on a dozen Lors to finish the roof on the place I'm building.' Lors are inhabitants of an impoverished province in eastern Iran, Lorestan. Hordes of them come to the capital, prepared to take on any sort of work.

'Congratulations, Madjid. You're building something, then?'

'Yes.'

'Where is your building?'

'Oh, it wouldn't be your sort of thing, Doctor *djan*. It's not worthy of you. It's a little six storey building in Madjidiyeh.'

'All the same . . . *khob, khob*, go on.'

'One of these Lors didn't know how to handle cement and got his face too close to the mixer. Both his eyes were burned. I took him straight to casualty but they said it was already too late. Now he's asking me for twelve million *tomans* in damages and at least one eye.'

I convert the sum into euros in my head: it's about twelve thousand at the day's rate.

My medical knowledge is limited and, therefore, not up

to knowing whether it's possible to graft an eye on to someone who has been badly burned and lost his sight. All the same, I still don't move. The world could fall apart and I wouldn't leave. Everything's happening here on the pavement outside the Central Passport Office at this exact moment with a doctor and a property developer discussing the transfer of an eye. I don't want to miss any of it. I'm not calling Nargess. Definitely.

'I've managed to get the twelve million *tomans* together,' Madjid goes on. 'It's been difficult, but I've got it now. But *Doctor djan* – "may I sacrifice myself for your fine face alone" – without you and without this eye I'll go to prison.'

'You crook, *agha* Madjid! Well done you, *sad afarins*. I mean, really. I kill myself working and struggling to earn a crust while you, my boy, you can get twelve million together in less than twenty-four hours.'

'I borrowed it! I've put my poor building up as surety! I've even sold it off in lots in advance!'

'How much did you ask per square metre?'

'One million two hundred thousand *tomans*.'

'That much? In Madjidiyeh?'

'*Doctor djan*, I bought it off-plan from a cousin, do you see? He took on an architect to build it, a man who qualified in Spain.'

'So?'

Suddenly, this isn't about an eye any more, or the blind Lors builder who came from his harsh native province with dreams of a better life at the back of his mind. It's all about the construction industry.

'When it's finished,' Madjid says, 'I'll invite you to come and see the building. I've never been to Spain myself but people who have, like *agha* Amir the butcher, say my building looks like things they saw there.'

I don't know which part of Spain the butcher *agha* Amir can have been to or what he's comparing Madjid's building to. Barcelona's Sagrada Familia? The Alhambra? The Bilbao Museum? I picture a replica of Gaudí's Pedrera looming up out of the working-class streets of Madjidiyeh. To be honest, that wouldn't surprise me now. Tehran has become a hotchpotch of buildings thrown up by irresponsible architects. A display of non-inspiration, a pot-pourri of the worst possible edifices scattered about the place. Opposite my apartment block, for example, there's a building which goes up in blocks of two storeys done in different styles. So the first and second have sculpted columns modelled on Persepolis with, on the façade, a (simplified) reproduction of the fêted Achaemenid soldiers with their curly hair and aquiline noses. The third and fourth storeys are graced by wooden balconies which, goodness knows why, evoke chalets in Switzerland or Austria. Tubs of geraniums hang from the windows, posing a constant threat to powerless passers-by. The fifth and sixth storeys are reminiscent of a New York loft, the seventh and eighth a Japanese temple. Finally, the ninth floor culminates in a vaguely Egyptian pyramid.

Even in the Shah's day, Tehran wasn't a very interesting capital. Its history only goes back to the thirteenth century and the Qadjar dynasty – a time when it became clear that Iranian art and civilisation were falling apart. Even the few ancient buildings in Tehran have nothing special about them compared to the timeless, moving edifices in Isfahan, Shiraz and Yazd, to name but a few. When a fashionable architect once showed me his latest masterpiece – a thirty-storey tower block – I remember noticing with some surprise that all the rooms had acute-angled corners: it was impossible to put a bed or sofa against any of the walls.

He confessed, not without pride, that he had overcome enormous difficulties in conceiving – he said 'creating' – that building.

'I didn't have any true inspiration,' he told me, 'until I hit on the idea of a butterfly. You see, my dear Nahal, the tower's designed on butterfly wings.'

'Really?'

I regretted, although I didn't say so, that it wasn't simply based on a human habitation, whatever shape it may have been. And I don't think butterflies ever came to see the place.

Even though they were ugly enough, the buildings constructed in the Shah's day were never more than ten storeys high, and houses in residential areas, buried in vast gardens, were usually discreet. Southern Tehran was poor, the centre administrative and the north rich. The Revolution didn't really alter this distribution. Change has come from overpopulation: in thirty years the capital's population has gone from three to twelve million. As result, what was once called the north has become almost the centre. Today's north has sprawled over the Alborz mountains, which dominates the city and now has concrete clambering over it. The west almost merges into the holiday resort of Karadj, and the south goes all the way to the gates of Behesht Zahra cemetery where martyrs of the Iran–Iraq war are laid to rest and, more importantly, where the mausoleum of Imam Khomeyni stands.

Nowadays, in the northern districts, it's rare to come across the sort of real gardens there were in my childhood, with wide driveways and ponds. Those large white houses built in the 1940s were either confiscated by the Islamic regime or sold off to building developers who first felled the huge old trees then – in a space once occupied by a family of five with two or three servants –

built a twenty-storey tower intended for four hundred inhabitants. The narrow streets previously used by the four or five residents' cars now have to cope with more than two thousand cars a day (unless my calculations are wrong), and that's only counting the houses actually on each street. And if on a Thursday evening (the equivalent of Saturday evening in the West), one of these lucky inhabitants decides to have a party at home, you have to multiply the amount of traffic and vehicles parking by five or six.

In this anarchic frenzy of building everyone threw in their own share of bad taste. I'll never forget a comment my mother made: "Tehran's finally become beautiful because at least now there's a harmony to its ugliness. Everything is uniformly ugly.' And she was right there. She was rarely wrong.

The Madjidiyeh area is to the east of Tehran. At the time our chauffeur lived there, and the only time I've ever been there was to go to his sister's wedding one autumn afternoon. The streets were narrow and full of boys 'with fragile necks, thin legs and knotted hair', as our great poetess Forough says. Women in chadors were heading home from shopping, red plastic baskets in hand. Girls in blue uniforms and with their hair loose rang their doorbells after a full day of school. The Madjidiyeh of today, with Gaudí's Pedrera in the middle of it (and why not?), probably also boasts a Pei 'Pyramid' and a Piano 'Pompidou Centre'. And goodness knows what else.

'I hope that by the time your building's finished,' Dâryoush says to the man looking for an eye, 'I'll be able to get together enough money to buy something the size of a dog kennel from you.'

'Everything I have is yours, doctor. But the units I've

got left aren't right for you. They're only between one and two hundred square metres.'

'You haven't got a little duplex, then?'

'Doctor *djan*, I do have one. But it's for the children.'

When he says 'the children' he actually means his wife. It is indecent for a traditional practising Muslim from his walk of life to refer directly to his wife. The word itself isn't used. So every time 'children' are mentioned you have to interpret this as meaning wife.

'*Basheh, basheh*. Of course. But next time you build a place, think of your poor lowly doctor, struggling to earn a living.'

'My children are your humble servants. They are the dust beneath your feet. Doctor *djan*, get me an eye, I beg you.'

Dâryoush looks at me again. One step ahead of him, I say, '*Force majeure*.'

He beckons me to follow him over to the scribes' car-desks, and asks them for some paper to write on. They don't have any. He makes Madjid buy a passport renewal form – still just as expensive – and on the back he gets one of the scribes to write out his request to Dr Sahabi. He signs the document and hands it to Madjid, who bends almost to the ground and kisses his benefactor's hand. I wonder secretly whether this letter is worth the price of a duplex in Madjidiyeh.

At that rate, how much would my passport renewal cost? A new van? Or why not a motorhome?

Madjid leaves and Dâryoush and I are back outside the gates. It's eleven o'clock. I head for the women's cloak-room: since the Revolution there's been a compulsory clothes check at the entrance to all administrative premises. Usually it's two or three severely veiled women sitting waiting to glance at the contents of visitors' handbags, closely inspect their faces and hands (which must have no make-up or nail varnish on them), and check the length of their trousers, coats and sleeves.

Early on in the Revolution it was a real ordeal getting through these cloakrooms. The inspectors, women who had the power to refuse us entry, came from the least favoured echelons of society and the Revolution had granted them the huge privilege of abusing us. They could have their revenge at last. Just belting a coat at the waist earned a volley of insults, 'Where are you from? Who brought you up? Didn't anyone teach you how to behave?'

In fact, that was all we ever were taught but there was no question of answering back. We had to look down, loosen the coat and leave as quickly as possible. Gradually, over time, the inspectors spent longer searching through handbags and took more interest in their contents than in visitors' make-up.

'Oh, your lipstick's a lovely colour,' one of them said once.

I immediately offered her the tube, feeling that this gesture won me back part – a very small part, granted – of my lost supremacy.

After almost thirty years of Islamic regime, the inspectors are still here. They are obviously another generation: the early ones lost their brothers in the Iran–Iraq war and married opium addicts whose only ambition is to have a satellite dish and watch Indian soaps. Today's inspectors are more smiley. So are we. They no longer resent us, we're not the ones responsible for their hardships. We talk to each other normally, without aggression, and even if they ask us to take off our nail varnish – with the help of a bit of acetone and some cotton wool that they keep in a drawer somewhere – they do it against their will, because they are paid to, because life is expensive, because their children don't have any shoes, because a chicken costs at least three thousand *tomans*, because they have forgotten what meat tastes like.

That pause, those few minutes it takes to inspect my clothes, can even bring us together, give us a peculiar sense of solidarity – them striving frantically to raise the money to educate their children and me coming back again and again, to various places like this, trying in vain to reclaim hundreds of hectares of land.

At the moment the three inspectors are dealing with a woman who has fainted.

'They've decided to settle things and this is what happens! A woman fainting and an old man dying,' announces one of them.

I notice that now these women also say 'they' when referring to 'them'.

'Drink, my darling. Have a mouthful of water,' suggests another, lifting the woman's head while the latter gesticulates to me to loosen her scarf.

Am I allowed to? I ask the inspectors for permission. They grant it.

'Of course! Take her scarf off, it's throttling her. They throttle us all,' the third one adds.

I don't say anything. I'm at the Central Passport Office. A mere nod from me could cost me an outright ban on leaving Iranian soil. Being cautious, I loosen the woman's scarf (rather than removing it) and wish her a speedy recovery. Then I open my handbag and show it to one of the inspectors, who doesn't even look at it or my make-up and clothes but lets me step through into the world of men, raising a curtain which inevitably smells of *shanbelileh*.

I meet up with Dâryoush in the internal courtyard. As he comes over to me he raises and lowers his fingers on a level with his eyes to tell me I need to lower my scarf. I do as I'm told.

'You're not slightly depressed, are you?' he asks.

'I'm very well. Don't worry about me. There's nothing like that.'

'I really ought to examine you sometime, though. You haven't got toothache?'

'No. Everything's fine.'

'I'll explain: the day before yesterday I was with a friend who had terrible toothache. I sent him to have an electro-cardiogram and saved him from a heart attack.'

I think about all the people around me with dental problems who should possibly be rushing to have check-ups in cardiology units. How many lives could be saved . . .

We go up the stairs of Building A and stop at a counter on the second floor. Lieutenants in police uniform with forage caps and decorative insignia sit the other side of a glass screen. In front of each window on the visitors' side, there is a school chair with a desk but they are lined up in such a way that visitors have to keep turning their heads to talk to the officers. A fat woman having difficulty shoe-horning her bulk into the narrow curve of the chair gives up the struggle. The windows along the counter are very low and, in order to talk to the policeman, she has to bend right down to knee level, affording everyone the view of two big fat buttocks – a spectacle, according to Islam, that warrants imprisonment for its perpetrator.

Further along a man of about forty is busy insulting Iran, his own country. 'I've come back home after twenty-five years away!' he bellows. 'I've got three doc-torates! I left everything behind – my villa, my cars, my job as a consultant pharmacologist – to come back and serve my country. And this is how "they" welcome us! That's it now! As soon as I get out I won't ever think about this bloody place again! I'll wipe it from my mind!'

As he passes us, Dâryoush blurts, 'You took your time seeing sense.'

Buttocks in the air, one hand on her back, the other on her knee, the fat woman asks the officer to repeat the same sentence three times.

'Your photograph doesn't look anything like you,' the official tells her.

'*Tchi*? What? But it was taken last week!' she rails.

She drops to the floor, takes a colour ID photo from a plastic sleeve and shows it to me.

'Does it look like me or doesn't it?' she asks me.

The photo has been touched up so much that the shading on the woman's face makes her look almost bony. I don't say anything but help her up, thinking about my own photo – the one of a woman at least ten years younger than me.

Dâryoush points at a free window: my turn has come. I settle myself on the desk chair and say good morning to the officer, a colonel, turning my head forty-five degrees towards him. I'm worried about the torments of a crick neck I'm likely to get if this meeting goes on long. Dâryoush stays standing, his small size in keeping with the furniture in the room. He says hello to the colonel and offers him his condolences, which doesn't surprise me: in Iran everyone's always mourning someone. Then he explains my situation. The colonel, whose beard comes right up to his eyes, utters just one sentence:

'Go to the office in Yaft Abad and ask for Lieutenant Mokhtarpour.'

Dâryoush sketches a military salute by way of a reply. Before we leave, though, the colonel who seems to be choking in his own beard asks Dâryoush, 'Askarnia *djan*, where have you got to with the body?'

Dâryoush goes up to the window and mutters something I don't hear.

My little voice and my rational self (which generally go hand in hand) conclude that Dâryoush must work for the morgue. He really is a doctor, that much is certain, but probably a pathologist. As such he must work closely with the police. Hence his contacts at the Ministry for the Interior.

But what's the connection with the Central Passport Office? my little voice asks. Since when have the dead needed passports?

I don't listen to it at all – my little voice is easily silenced. My blood pressure dives again. As there are only two of us this time, I can have my caramel. I offer one to Dâryoush, who accepts eagerly.

We go down into the courtyard and I leave through the women's cloakroom. I wave to the three inspectors who are eating bread and cheese, and to the woman who fainted and now seems better. The inspectors offer me some of their food. Out of habit, in keeping with *tarof*, I say no. But I slow down and admit I would like a mouthful because I've got blood pressure problems. They immediately offer me a chair. One of them pours me a glass of tea, another hands me some bread and cheese.

I sit amongst them. A visitor just coming in shows me her handbag: I glance at it and let her through.

Worried because I haven't reappeared, Dâryoush calls from outside. I quickly drain my cup of tea and thank the inspectors before leaving.

'Yaft Abad here we come,' the doctor says as I join him. All I know about the Yaft Abad district is that it is in the very south of Tehran. In the Shah's day it housed the poorest of the poor in what amounted to slums. Getting there nowadays, with all the traffic congestion, is something of an expedition. When Dâryoush suggests taking me there in his van I tell him my *ajans* is waiting and the driver will take me to Yaft Abad himself.

Considering it a waste of my money to keep the car, Dâryoush launches into endless calculations to prove it's cheaper to take three taxis than stay with the same one for the whole day. I let him get on with it. Everyone has their own way of running their money. We walk over to his van side by side. He throws his attaché case in the back, then sits at the wheel and tugs on the seat belt but doesn't do it up. I tell him there's no hurry, he has plenty of time to put it on properly.

'Oh no!' he says. 'I don't put it on, I just wedge it between my knees.'

'Why?'

'Because if I'm stopped, it's not like I haven't put it on at all. It's negotiable, specially with my contacts . . .'

'But why don't you put it on?' I insist.

'*Azis-e delam*, oh precious to my heart, when death comes for us nothing can stop it, and certainly not a seat belt made God knows where.'

'But you could be injured, you could break a rib or your nose . . .'

Dâryoush shows me his forehead and declares, 'That depends on what fate has written here. If you have to have a leg amputated, here or anywhere else, it'll take its dues.'

He moves off with his seat belt clamped between his

thighs and idles slowly over to my *ajans* to give the driver the address of the passport office in Yaft Abad, recommending that he follows him.

We set off. From the side, I can see my driver nervously nibbling the ends of his moustache and periodically twitching his right shoulder. Something is bothering him.

After two or three minutes he can't hold out any longer.

'I'm from Yaft Abad myself,' he tells me. 'You know it's pretty demeaning for me to follow this guy in his battered van to get there.'

'Not at all. Doctor Askarnia (I emphasise the "doctor") had no intention of upsetting you. He didn't know you were from Yaft Abad. How could he have known? It was just to help me out, so we could avoid traffic jams.'

The driver goes on champing his moustache.

'Well, if I agree to be led,' he concedes, 'it's only for your sake.'

I thank him for his selflessness. We submerge ourselves in an ocean of cars, some of which look like models from *Mad Max*. In the course of their lives they change size, height and shape several times. The most common model is the national car, the Peykan, and wherever you go you can't help hearing people comparing its price 'in the old days' and 'now': 'in the old days, under the Shah, a Peykan cost thirty thousand *tomans*, now it'll set you back six and a half million.' Taxes on new vehicles are very high – ninety per cent – so people change cars by buying them second-hand. Iran is therefore the only country to my knowledge where a second-hand car that's been used for a good ten years and covered hundreds of thousands of kilometres can be sold for more than its original price. I've even witnessed the sale of a car wreck which fell into a ravine after an accident but still fetched more that its initial price.

Nargess, who's more clued up about everything than me, never stops urging me to invest in cars.

'You buy a Peugeot made in Iran. You leave it in the car park under your building for a year, then you sell it on for thirty per cent more. Wouldn't you call that a good investment?' she says at least once a week.

I'm happy the traders on Wall Street (still Wall Street!) can't hear Nargess. Otherwise they would all be rushing to Iran to buy 'Iranian' Peugeots, leave them in my parking space and sell them off a year later.

In recent years Tehran has also acquired Mercedes (which Iranians call Benz), Ferraris and Porsches which their owners buy – I have to reiterate – with ninety per cent tax. When these travelling treasures pass in the street, wherever you happen to be, you are therefore bound to hear the litany: 'Look at those sons of ayatollahs in their Porsches, see how rich they've become.'

If you look closely there's nothing 'sons of ayatollahs' about them. They look like the gilded youth of any other country, accompanied by pretty girls (with a few wisps of blonde hair peeping out from under their scarves) and listening to the latest hits, sometimes even decadent Western music, which is forbidden. All the same, anyone you ask would assure you they really are the sons or grandsons of ayatollahs and the source of terrible torment to their honourable grandfathers. There are rumours about the city that the granddaughter of one be-turbaned high-ranking official has been arrested several times by the Revolutionary Guard for her lack of respect for Islamic dress.

We take a succession of different motorways running the

length of Tehran. They bear the names of generals from the Iran–Iraq war, names no one but the military head-quarters recognises, which stirs up constant discord between the Shah's partisans, those who defend the Republic and sceptics. The first group say plans for these motorways were drawn up under the imperial regime, the second claim it was the mullahs now in power who devised them, and the third insist that, whether they are the work of the Shah or the mullahs, the motorways don't do any-thing to ease the huge traffic jams that paralyse Tehran. The city turns into a giant car park at rush hour every day.

After an hour and a half spent inhaling a more than negligible amount of carbon dioxide, we reach Yaft Abad. I was expecting slums, hovels of sheet metal, crumbling shacks, cardboard boxes used as homes. To my astonish-ment, I find a place more pleasant than northern Tehran, complete with tree-lined boulevards, green spaces and even cultural centres. Nargess and various other people have actually told me that the south of the city had become very nice but I didn't believe them. This transformation has come about because, thanks to an exceptional budget, the governing powers have put an unusual amount of effort into improving living conditions in these suburbs. During the Iran–Iraq war they supplied the largest contin-gent of martyrs.

From time to time I let my eye linger discreetly on my driver, and it looks to me as if his moustache has been so chewed that it is actually shorter. He agreed, against his own better judgement, to follow the little man in the van and he can't bear it.

All of sudden he brakes and clamps his hands on the steering wheel.

'*Khanoum*, I'm stopping here,' he says. 'He's been round

this square twice now and I've had to follow him. People know me here, do you see what I mean, it's humiliating for me to drive round a square twice, here, where I come from.'

I notice that the top section of his index finger is missing. He twitches his shoulder and waits for my reply.

He called me *khanoum*, a polite form of address to a woman. By saying this simple word, he deserves to overtake all the other cars, not only in his own part of the city but in all of Iran and even in Paris. Since the Revolution, Islamic custom has forced men to call young women 'sister' and the not so young 'mother', or '*hadj khanoum*', an honorary title that means someone of the female sex who has made a pilgrimage to Mecca.

As a result, overnight, my mother and every woman of her generation were addressed as *madar* (which means 'mother') in any office, shop or restaurant. Once when a waiter handed my mother a menu and called her *madar* she retorted, 'But I've never slept with your father! How can I be your mother?' The waiter flicked a look of surprise at this woman who hadn't slept with his father but whom he now had to call *madar*, before slipping back to the kitchen without a word.

My mother, her again, also refused to be called *hadj khanoum*. Being very familiar with history and Islamic vocabulary, if someone like the man at the pâtisserie – for example – called her *hadj khanoum*, she would respond in Arabic, telling him it was forbidden to abuse that title by assigning it to someone who had never seen the Kaaba, as she herself had not. This instantly dampened the enthusiasm of the unfortunate pâtisserie chef handing her his cream puffs.

Nargess, who is a few years older than me, dreads the

time when she will go from *khadar*, 'sister' to *madar*, 'mother'. I share this fear, as do all women my age.

I call Dâryoush on his mobile. He stops and says he's looking for a petrol station, which explains his detours. I ask my driver to show us where there's a garage. He shrugs his shoulders again, but this time he twiddles his moustache between his fingers and – revealing a golden tooth – announces proudly, 'Tell him to follow me, madam.'

We go round the square a third time. The driver winds down his window and calls to a passer-by, 'The little guy in the van back there thought he could make fun of me in my own neighbourhood. If madam wasn't here . . .'

I think to myself that the driver must be a member of a *loutis*, shady organisations with their own code of honour, special language and distinctive customs. In the Shah's days they were called *kolah makhmalis*, 'velvet hats'. They wore black suits over open-neck white shirts, and of course the famous hats, the *kolah makhmalis*. Popular films from before the Revolution, aping American cinema with its Italian Mafia, made them its heroes of choice. In real life, just like in films, these men had their own families, but what singled them out and gave them irresistible charm was the self-destructive love they inevitably had for some beautiful prostitute. They would take these women out to the cabarets of the day, while their wives stayed walled up at home. They fought valiantly for them and, for the rest of their lives, bore scars from the blows received in trying to defend a forsaken woman's honour.

I've always had a soft spot for their vocabulary. A man only has to talk to me the way they do, with that look in his eye, that intonation, and I melt. The Revolution had swept away the cabarets, drinking sessions, fights erupting over a beauty spot above a call-girl's lip, but also, I'm not sure why, the *kolah makhmalis* themselves, even though they were practising Muslims. Granted, they drank alcohol and danced sensuously but they said twice as many prayers to be sure of absolution, and they fasted all through Ramadan, never succumbing – even after nightfall – to a single drop of the dangerous drink they called *aragh sagui*, 'dog arak'.

Knowing I took an interest in them and their sudden disappearance, a painter friend of mine who had been a Revolutionary Guard told me they had been decimated by the war. Being men of honour, they all volunteered to fight on the front and very few came back. Their successors, also descended from the underprivileged sector of society, found something similar to the solidarity that had united them in the ranks of the *pasdarans*, the Revolutionary Guard – the only difference being that the latter now symbolised Islamic law and had lost for ever any notion of fantasy. My friend has several of those velvet hats hanging in his studio, the vestiges of a time which now felt long gone.

He himself was the very image of that vanished caste, that band of outlaws which metamorphosed peculiarly into pure Revolutionary Guards. I felt my friend was trying to preserve the traces of former escapades in his painter's palette.

We wait for Dâryoush outside the petrol station. He has barely paid for his fuel before the driver with the truncated finger (knife fight, war wound?) tells me, 'Now it's his turn to follow me.'

This is non-negotiable. I know that. I put my head out of the window and call to Dâryoush, 'Doctor, please follow us! My driver lives in Yaft Abad and knows exactly where the passport office is.'

'Why didn't you say so in the first place? I would have followed you blindly,' retorts Dâryoush.

The driver twiddles his moustache between his fingers again and raises his right shoulder.

'I'm at your disposal,' he replies. 'I am your servant. I have to follow you.'

I feel light-headed and satisfied. An altercation has been avoided and I've saved a man's pride.

The car suddenly stops in the middle of the boulevard.

'Get out, madam,' the driver says without looking round. 'I can't go any further. I'm going to turn round and wait for you in one of those streets back there.'

I sit up in my seat and look out. There seems to be a huge piece of black fabric covering the street – fabric that has countless holes, affording glimpses of arms and faces. It is in fact hundreds of women, all in black chador, sitting silently on the ground, in the street. Immediately I think this must be some sort of demonstration against the United States or Israel.

Dâryoush raps on the window and asks me to get out.

'Where are we going?'

'The same as them, the Yaft Abad passport office,' he says.

'Are they waiting for passports?'

'Of course.'

Until now my only source of satisfaction rested in the fact that the inhabitants of Yaft Abad – poor, hard-working people – surely couldn't be big on requesting passports. I therefore thought we wouldn't have to stand in an endless queue here, as you do everywhere else.

Dâryoush soon sets me straight.

'It's worse here than anywhere else.'

'Worse? Why?'

'Because they all want to go to Karbala.'

Karbala in Iraq is the sacred town of Shiites, where Imam Hosseyn, the Prophet's grandson, is laid to rest. In Shiite mythology Hosseyn is the incarnation of the king of martyrs, never hesitating to expose his own life and that of his family and his seventy-two companions, to the oppressor's cruel sabres. They were betrayed and slaughtered at Karbala. The tragedy of their death is the founding text of the Shiite faith.

The Persian empire of the Sassanides, which stretched from India to Egypt, was conquered by the Arabs in the seventh century and brutally broken up. Iranians, who had professed Zoroastrianism until then, were forced to convert to Islam. The Caliphate built Baghdad on the ruins of Ctesiphon, the Sassanides' capital. Far from being annihilated, the Persian civilisation took on Islamic dress, enriched its conquerors' culture with its own glorious past and dazzled in every field of so-called Islamic achievement: science, philosophy, architecture and painting.

The Shiite faith, which the Sunnis see as heresy, is based on a refusal to accept Abou Bakr, the first Caliph, as the Prophet's successor. The Shiites have chosen Ali, the Prophet's son-in-law, as his true heir, and Ali's descendants – the Imams – as sole representatives of worldly power. Other than in Imams' hands, any power is illegitimate, abusive, corrupt or unjust. Fighting it, as Hosseyn did when he rebelled against the Caliph, is the recurring theme of a Shiite's life. The cycle of Imams, the legitimate pretenders to the power abusively exercised by the Caliphs, concludes with the twelfth Imam, the hidden Imam, the Mehdi who has voluntarily withdrawn from sight but will redress centuries of injustice when he reappears.

To distinguish themselves from the Arabs, Iranians have

adopted Shiism as their own brand of Islam, and the Prophet's grandson Imam Hosseyn as their chosen hero.

Every year during the month of *moharam*, the month of his death, the whole of Iran goes into mourning. They celebrate this passion with ceremonies involving self-flagellation, funeral chants, offerings of food, nocturnal processions, and theatrical productions (*tazieh*) most of which are performed outdoors. Even in the Shah's day I can remember my mother dragging us off to Sar Tcheshmeh in 'Old Tehran', the neighbourhood where she was brought up, where a family who still adhered to tradition celebrated the Imam's death according to old customs. Their small garden heaved with crowds of mourners. Two huge pots filled the penitents' bellies with rice and the best *khoresht-e gheymeh* I've ever eaten. A mullah recited the passion of Hosseyn and listeners, gathered in separate groups of men and women, wept, some clawing their faces, others beating their chests. Each of them recognised in the Imam's martyrdom the injustices of his or her own life and, over and above any individual experience, the tragedy of the human condition.

On beyond the house was a small temple, about three metres by two, reached down a short flight of steps. It was called the Haft Dokhtaroum and was usually dark and deserted, but on that day was illuminated by a myriad candles lit by hands asking for a son's good health, a reduction in a husband's debts, a brother's release and all sorts of other earthly favours.

The Islamic Revolution used and abused the cult of martyrs to consolidate its own foundations and then defend Iran against the Iraqi invasion. Without the Imam Hosseyn, and the deeply entrenched cult of martyrdom, young Iranians would not have volunteered. Without the

Imam Hosseyn, Saddam would have conquered Iran. In fact it is precisely since Saddam's downfall that Iranians have at last been able to go to Iraq and visit Hosseyn's mausoleum in Karbala. I sometimes think, given the choice between a pilgrimage to Mecca or Karbala, an Iranian would prefer the latter, hence the sheer size of this tide of black now covering the tarmac of the Martyrs' Boulevard in Yaft Abad.

To get into the passport office you either have to trample over these women in their black chador or effect balletic leaps to avoid them. I choose to tread on them, offering apologies with every step. Some get to their feet to stand in my way, protesting that they've been here twenty-four hours. But Dâryoush, who has managed to reach the policeman on duty at the door and have a few words with him, is pointing at me and asking for me to be let through. The policeman seems to give his permission. The women sit back down and we go into the building.

Inside, the resistance is more serious. Men and women snake all the way up the stairs to the second floor where the counters are. Though small, Dâryoush doesn't succeed in worming his way through.

'I need to see Lieutenant Mokhtarpour in person!' he calls to a police officer blocking the way between the first and second floors. 'Lieutenant Mokhtarpour!'

The officer can't hear him. Dâryoush does manage to make his way gradually up to him, just by repeating the manager's name. I stay rooted to the spot. From below I can see Dâryoush arguing with the police officer, who proves more difficult to convince than the first. Faced with Dâryoush's insistence and the jostling visitors, he eventually gives in and lets him through. Dâryoush waves at me to come up. Quickly! But how? Here, even balletic leaps wouldn't help. In order to get to the first floor I would have to achieve one huge perilous jump or glide through the air as in martial arts films. In an attempt to extricate me from the depths, Dâryoush reaches out his hand. I barge past people, still apologising, pointing to Dâryoush and climbing slowly and with some difficulty up the staircase. At last I reach the first floor.

'It's as if you haven't got any hands and feet! You're so weak! Believe me, you really should have some blood tests. I've been waiting half an hour up here for you! You won't get far if you're always so timid.'

I can actually feel my blood pressure dropping again. But I know I don't have any more sweets. I don't say anything. Dâryoush walks into the big hall on the first floor, goes over to Lieutenant Mokhtarpour's office and asks to see him.

'Everyone in this place wants to see Lieutenant Mokhtarpour,' his male secretary replies without even looking up. 'Go back down to the ground floor and wait your turn.'

I turn meekly to go back downstairs. Dâryoush can't grab my hand (all physical contact being forbidden) so he yells, 'Where do you think you're going? Don't move a muscle! Oh, these depressives! Don't move!'

He walks round the police officer, whispers something in his ear then, very clearly, writes his name on a page in the diary lying on the desk, tears the page out and hands it to the man.

'On my head be it! Take that to the lieutenant! Quick!' he bellows.

The secretary gets up from his desk (beneath which I notice a pair of plastic child's slippers), heads slowly for the lieutenant's office and comes back a few minutes later saying we should wait there. The door to the office opens, and closes. People go in and come out. Each time, Dâryoush wants to go in. In vain. Eventually, although we don't know why, the secretary tells us we can cross the longed-for threshold.

Before we do, Dâryoush indicates that I should lower my rebellious scarf. I do as he says. He opens the door and immediately, still with his briefcase in his hand, gives a military salute. I catch myself raising my own arm, as a reflex, and bringing my heels together, but I pull myself together just in time and wait for Dâryoush's secret litany, the one he always seems to whisper in every boss's ear. Here we progress from a whisper to a cry as Detective Chief Inspector Mokhtarpour suggests we sit down.

But his office is only equipped with three chairs and they are already occupied by an old woman in chador, a clean-shaven young man and a woman in a red scarf. The young man stands up and gives me his chair, which I offer to Dâryoush. He asks me to sit down and explains, 'She's got very low blood pressure.'

At once the officer opens a drawer and takes out a box of pistachio-flavoured Isfahan nougat – something frequently recommended for low blood pressure. I take a piece and then, because he insists, a second. The three other visitors are indulged with the same treat (even if their blood pressure is through the roof!)

The old woman in chador, who can't stop fidgeting, launches into an endless enumeration of the officer's merits.

'If he weren't here,' she tells me, 'I'd still be on the list of people not allowed out of the country.'

The *mamnou ol-khorouj*, the 'forbidden to leave', are usually high-ranking members of the former regime or people who oppose the Islamic Republic. As I chew on my nougat I wonder how a *chadori* old woman could end up banned from leaving Iran.

'My son!' she wails at the officer, reaching her hands towards him. '*May God double the days of your life! May God grant that your children grow old!* You've saved me. Without you, who could have got a passport for Sweden? Who could have seen their own son?'

I think that had Mr Eskandari, our caretaker, been here he would definitely have taken his crumpled piece of paper from his pocket and given the old woman the last telephone number he has for his son who vanished in Sweden.

Why is Sweden so sought after? Because it is the chosen country for Iranian emigrants. Those tourists who refuse to leave when their visas run out are almost immediately put up in prefabricated houses with a view of the sea, or at least a lake. The Swedish government also provides them with a free telephone card to call home as often as they like. A special card opens the doors to Ikea for them so they can decorate their temporary houses to their own liking, and a psychologist sees them regularly, free of charge, to avoid any nostalgia spoiling their time in Scandinavia.

Acting on the advice of informed friends, an ageing Iranian woman from a modest background once told the psychologist that what she missed most in Sweden was her car and chauffeur. The very next day a Saab driven by Karl, a blond, blue-eyed chauffeur, was put at her disposal for two hours a day, at the government's expense.

While they wait for their papers to be regularised, 'illegal workers' are remunerated by the Ministry for Education so they can learn Swedish. In order to avoid this ordeal, the old woman – still on good advice from her friends – had to feign the symptoms of Alzheimer's. She could easily remember the past and driving along the Caspian coast but the present, Karl the chauffeur, the Saab and the daily trip from Svea Vägen to Gamla Stan meant absolutely nothing to her. The psychologists concluded that, as an exception, she could be excused lessons in Swedish.

Once their papers are regularised, immigrants carry on being paid, this time to learn a trade or to improve the skills they used in their home country. In the old woman's case, the 'Social' (the organisation responsible for taking over from the Ministry for Education) decreed that, given the individual's mental state, her salary could be paid without any need for training. She therefore continued to receive indemnities. But as she had worked all her life she started making food – not free of charge – for her chauffeur, then his friends, then his friends' friends. Inundated by the beautiful, the sublime specimens from the transport workers' union, who saw her as a guardian angel, she had, with great regret, to turn down this lucrative revenue and, with Karl's help, set up an Iranian fast-food restaurant right in the middle of town. Apparently, at lunchtime the queue of regulars winds all the way round the building. The King of Sweden himself has proved unable to resist the charms of her *koukou sabzi*, a herb omelette. Still on the recommendations of her well-informed friends, she had the words FAST FOOD THAT'S A LONG TIME COMING written above the door in Swedish.

I look at the old woman sitting beside me and picture her settled in Sweden, in partnership with the owner of the fast-food restaurant. All of a sudden, without any warning, she opens her chador and puts a live chicken on to Lieutenant Mokhtarpour's desk. The chicken's feet, wings and beak are bound, and it rolls over the officer's documents, struggling as best it can, squawking in terror (but quietly, thanks to the bound beak) and shedding feathers. When the chicken falls to the floor, the officer takes a couple of steps back.

'What on earth do you think you're doing?'

He has a northern accent, from Rasht. I'd like to confide in him that I'm from Mazandaran, the neighbouring province, to try and establish a bit of regional solidarity. But this isn't the moment. Far from refusing the old woman's gift, the lieutenant calls his secretary and instructs him to take the chicken to the staff car park. I can imagine him going home after work with a live chicken beneath his arm. He's from the north, he likes fresh produce, he can't resist the taste of a real chicken reared out of doors. I secretly wish I could tell him he's quite right, this chicken probably won't taste anything like a bird sold under cellophane. But I hold my tongue on that too: he might interpret the remark as an attempt at corruption. Caution.

The old woman bids her farewells to us all, praying everyone's affairs are settled as favourably as her own.

'*Elahi amin, amen,*' replies Dâryoush

He sits on the old girl's chair and points to the woman in the red scarf as he whispers in my ear, 'Now that one's pimping. She sends girls to Dubai.'

The woman in question has a lock of blonde hair showing beneath her scarf, painted toenails peeping out of her sandals with the profiles of a man and a woman drawn on them. Silicon-implanted lips and a Botoxed forehead complete the look.

As soon as it was instituted, the Islamic Republic cleared the red-light district, Shahr-e Now in the north of Tehran, a place devoted to satisfying males from the 'third class'. I recently saw a series of photos of the enclave taken in the 1970s. In one black and white shot a pot-bellied woman with her chador tied round her waist sits heavily on a lopsided chair. Close by, a cat slinks along a decrepit wall. A wheelbarrow full of soil stands in the middle of the room. All the photos emphasised the squalor and destitution of that way of life.

Meanwhile, men from the 'first class' assuaged their desires with ravishing blondes sent from Paris by Madame Claude. As for men from the 'second class', I'm not sure how they managed.

After Shahr-e Now was so virtuously destroyed and the Parisian charter flights teeming with blondes were stopped, men from the first and third class – secretly, I imagine – had to do what those from the second had done all along . . . whatever that was. Still, at some point in the 1990s girls with almond-shaped eyes, arched eyebrows and rosebud lips started appearing on the pavements of chic boulevards in Tehran (the capital of the Islamic Republic). Tricky to tell the difference between them and other girls waiting for taxis, except that, when they bend over to 'give the address', what they're really giving is their price. As everywhere else, this varies according to the weather and the performance required. I've heard that a weekend in the north can be negotiated up to a thousand dollars.

How much is that in euros? I privately wonder. I can't help myself, but don't give myself time to calculate it.

These girls come just as much from the third class as the second or first. Some want to enrol at university but don't have the money to pay their way. Others can only think of having their own car, a Pride – assembled in Iran and bought at twice its original value – so that their mothers no longer have to wait for the bus at five o'clock in the morning to get to work. For others, the constant longing to go to Europe warrants every sacrifice.

I don't know what category the girls with the woman in the red scarf belong to and, of course, daren't ask whether she's here to get passports for all of them. To each his own concerns.

She puts her elbows on the desk, looks the officer right in the eye (clearly forbidden behaviour) and drags her words as she speaks as if they were the train of a dress.

'My deeeear, Lieutenaaaaaant, I proooomise to light a huuuundred candles if you can teeeell me my problems are soooolved today.'

He makes a phone call, consults a file on his desk (which still has a few chicken feathers whirling over it) and sighs. The hundred candles won't be lit today. Yet again. He'll have to see. The young woman withdraws her elbow from the table.

'Tomorroooow? Can I come back tomorroooow?'

'Call before coming. Here's the office number.'

'Thaaaaank you from the bottom of my heaaaaaart.'

I can just see the lieutenant – with the live chicken under his arm – climbing into the Pride driven by this woman in a red scarf. I can see her lighting a hundred candles tomorrow. And so on and so forth.

She leaves and we're left with the clean-shaven young man (not keen to wear a beard even if that would make this easier for him).

'Right, on to you. Have you got your certificate for completing your military service?' asks the lieutenant.

The Military Service Organisation in Iran is an institution like no other. It is not corrupt. It never has been. In the Shah's day, and the same is true today, it was rare for a boy of recruitment age to get away without doing military service. I remember under the imperial system that bachelors – who had to produce the military service certificate before they could marry – were happier growing old far from their loved ones, in Switzerland or somewhere like that, and never coming back to Iran for fear of being forced to carry out their national service, which was an absolute obligation.

The war against Iraq only aggravated the situation. Every young man was sent to the front. In order to protect them, their parents liquidated all their assets: houses, cars, carpets and jewellery. They often smuggled their sons abroad, over the Turkish mountains or the Pakistani plains. Nowadays, young men in the first class – in other words the rich, the masters of the Islamic Republic – have even set a price on authorisations to come in and out of the country, in the full knowledge that, without the military service certificate, no young man can ever leave Iranian soil. Recalcitrant rich boys just have to pay the Military Service Organisation five thousand dollars for the doors of Mehrabad and Imam Khomeyni airports to open up before them as if by magic.

'Show it to me!' demands the lieutenant.

'I haven't got it on me,' answers the beardless young man.

'Well, get out of here and come back when your documents are in order. He thinks anything goes here,' the lieutenant adds, looking at Dâryoush.

'Go on then!' he says, turning back to the young man. 'I can't do anything for you.'

The young man says goodbye through pinched lips and slowly leaves the office.

'Now, Doctor *djan*, your turn. What can I do for you?'

'I've just come from Colonel Azardel at the Central Passport Office. He sends you many greetings.'

'He's our big boss.'

Someone knocks on the door. The lieutenant, slightly annoyed, calls them in. The same young man appears in the doorway and asks, 'What if I can't find my military service certificate?'

'Have you done your military service or not?' the lieutenant asks him, raising his voice.

'Of course I have.'

'Well, bring me the certificate.'

The young man closes the door.

'Perhaps you should call Colonel Azardel and give him your condolences,' Dâryoush goes on. 'You know, because his cousin . . .'

'Doctor *djan*, I was just about to ask you his mobile number but that obstinate creep who hasn't done his military service won't leave me alone.'

Dâryoush gives him the colonel's number on the spot. The door opens again and the clean-shaven young man reappears without being told to come in.

'Where can I get a duplicate of a military service certificate?' he asks cheekily.

'Try your great-aunt's cat!' cries the lieutenant. 'Close the door, I don't want to see you again!'

The young man disappears without another word. Dâryoush tells Lieutenant Mokhtarpour that an imminent conference in France means I can't wait a month for my new passport, that it's a very important symposium . . . that this . . . that that . . .

'Get up to the second floor quickly,' the lieutenant interrupts him. 'It's nearly two o'clock and then we close the counters.'

'My dear lieutenant, would your goodness stretch to asking your secretary to accompany us?'

'Doctor *djan, may my face be blackened*! I can't do that. You see, all those people queueing between the first and second floors have been waiting since the day before yesterday.'

'I won't ask again. But, if that's the case, would you have another couple of nougats for her?' asks Dâryoush.

The lieutenant hands me the box. Then, in a rush of kindness, he does actually call in his secretary and give him orders to facilitate our access to the second floor.

'Once there, they can queue at the counters for themselves,' he adds.

My blood pressure problems and Dâryoush's adroitness have just saved us at least an hour, perhaps a whole day. In the blink of an eye we get to the counters on the second floor where we do, finally, have to respect the queueing system like everyone else. There are three people waiting in front of us. We sit down on benches and, for the first time that day, I at last have an opportunity to talk to Dâryoush – or Dr Askarnia. We embark on a conversation but his mobile has been ringing constantly for some time now.

'Yes, I couldn't care less, it's not my fault,' he tells the caller, 'he just should have revised better.' Then turning back to me, 'Have you known *agha* Morad long?'

Agha Morad is none other than the photographer from the Ecbatana studio, the one who put me in touch with this doctor who looks like Dâryoush. I don't know what to say. Admitting the truth – when I'm within reach of the passport issuing desk – could be a fatal mistake.

'*Agha* Morad and his colleague Hassan *agha* are very helpful,' I say cautiously. 'Everyone in my neighbourhood talks about how kind they are.'

'*Agha* Morad's brother is a colleague of mine at the University of Law.'

His mobile rings again.

'Akbari? Wait and I'll check,' Dâryoush replies.

He opens his briefcase, leafs briefly through a notebook and announces, 'Akbari didn't reach the pass mark, he'll have to come back in September.'

Dâryoush ends the call.

'I usually give a class at the University of Law at two o'clock.'

'Oh really? What do you teach?'

'Criminology. But my love for *agha* Morad's brother and for *agha* Morad himself means that, in order to help you out, I can't get to my class. That's why my students keep ringing me, you see? They want to know their marks.'

I thank him and wonder privately what this 'helping out' is going to cost me. I also wonder what sort of fees a pathologist gets if he skips his own lessons to take an acquaintance of a brother of a friend to the passport office in Yaft Abad.

His mobile rings again. The doctor listens and eventually cries out with some vehemence, 'I've told him a hundred times not to miss lessons! But he won't listen to me, he never comes! Yes, yes, I know, I know. His brother was a martyr, so what? That still doesn't mean I can pile marks on for him.'

Clearly irritated, he gets to his feet, heads over towards the counter and carries on his verbal resistance. I feel like telling him he should gratify the martyr's brother with a good mark in spite of his shortcomings. Who knows, it might just speed up my application for a national ID card – the fêted *kart-e melli* – or (you never know) help me reclaim my land in the north some day. Well, we all have our dreams.

Dâryoush comes and sits back down.

'They won't give up,' he explains. 'Let's get back to *agha* Morad. Do you know his brother?'

'No, I've never met him.'

'Well, you've missed half your life. He's one of those *khosh typ*, one of those good-looking boys they just don't make any more. At the University of Law they called him Alain Delon. Do you know who Alain Delon is?'

I nod shyly. I don't tell him my husband wrote two of his films, *Borsalino* and *The Swimming Pool*. That could all get too involved.

'Apparently he divorced Brigitte Bardot.'

'Really? I didn't know about that.'

Nor do I say that my husband wrote *Viva Maria* and knew Bardot, a long time ago now. Stars seem to grow old more slowly here than anywhere else. But I'd do better not to talk about them. Too much risk of being sidetracked.

'You know, *inshallah*, I'm going to tell you something. Once you've got your passport and you've got over the other side, don't come back to Iran. Listen to your doctor. Listen to me even though I'm not that much older than you.'

He takes my passport, opens it and reads my date of birth.

'Just as I thought. We're five years apart. Yes, as I was saying, once you're there, don't come back, ask for citizenship. I've got Romanian nationality, you know.'

I don't tell him that I also have French nationality, and even a French passport, which I prefer not to use here. His mobile rings. He's stopped answering it.

'I moved my wife and children – two little girls, pretty as dolls – to Romania.'

'I send them everything I earn. I don't keep any of it here. None.'

'Do you speak Romanian?'

'Of course not. But my wife and children speak it fluently, you can be sure of that.'

It's our turn. We go up to the counter and a man in uniform checks my documents. I'm worried he won't accept my photos but they don't seem to be a problem. He hasn't even looked at me. Then he suddenly hands the whole application back to us saying, 'Come back tomorrow, you haven't got photocopies of pages one to ten.'

'I'll do them straight away!' Dâryoush replies.

'No, we're closing, it's three o'clock. I'm supposed to leave at two.'

'It'll only take a minute! I'll nip down and do them in Lieutenant Mokhtarpour's office.'

'His photocopier's not working.'

'But madam has been given a recommendation from the very top. *Oh, may I die!* Just give me a minute to go and get these photocopies!'

'Run, then. Go on, run!'

Dâryoush grabs my passport and waves me after him. We thunder down the stairs, perhaps not four at a time but at least two at a time.

The police officer on the first floor is busy sending away all the visitors. We go out with them and Dâryoush tells the policeman on the ground floor to wait for us before locking the door.

'She won't forget the cake,' he whispers in his ear. This means I'll have to pay the policeman. I nod agreement. I suggest getting the *ajans* driver to help with the photocopying.

'He's a local. He'll do it quickly.'

Dâryoush refuses and replies, not without pride, 'I won't entrust this passport to anyone.'

He tramples yet again over the dozens of women sitting on the ground waiting their turn until tomorrow or the day after. He hands me his briefcase, clamps my passport between his teeth, probably so as not to lose it en route, and gets into his van. He sets off and I watch him leave. I can see his profile with the passport jutting out between his nose and chin. I am now alone outside the passport office.

The policeman is watching me, waiting for his 'cake'. How much should I give him? I feel like calling Nargess. I take five one-thousand *tomans* notes from my bag and slip them discreetly into his hand. Our hands touch, thereby putting Islam at risk. He quickly stuffs the money into his pocket, without checking how much there is, and thanks me.

'It'll be forty degrees soon,' he adds, 'and I can't afford a fan for my family.'

I feel ashamed. I could have given him more, much more. Five thousand *tomans* is nowhere near enough to buy a fan.

'*Inshallah*,' I say, 'the day I come and pick up my passport, I'll pay for all the inconvenience I've caused you.' Which, in good Persian, means he'll have to wait till I come back before he can get his fan.

Time passes and still no Dâryoush. I wait patiently. The policeman starts fretting. If Dâryoush takes much longer, he'll be asking me for a fridge, a freezer, a microwave and God knows what else. My little voice, which has been stifled until now, expresses its concerns loudly and clearly: someone's taken my passport without giving me any sort of receipt. The policeman points at his watch.

'The doctor will be back any minute,' I tell him. Then I recite the script learned from Dâryoush, 'Lieutenant Mokhtarpour asked him to photocopy a letter that I have to give to Colonel Azardel myself.'

The names have their effect. The policeman nods his head, moves away slightly and turns away two or three women trying to get in.

'Come back tomorrow,' he tells them. 'We're not taking any more applications today, you can see that.'

One of them points at me and shrieks, 'What about her? What's she doing there? Why haven't you told her to go away too?'

'She's been sent from the very top.'

The woman comes right up to me as if to strike me. I take a few steps back.

'We didn't go through a Revolution so that women like you could get through before us!' she cries. 'I'll show you, I will. I'll show you all that sort of thing's finished . . . finished a long time ago.'

I'd like to be swallowed up into the bowels of the earth. I'd like to disappear. I'd like to be wandering happily through a department store, I'd like to buy a Marni jacket, I'd like to . . .

All at once I spot Dâryoush coming back, with the passport and photocopies between his teeth. We've got them. The application is complete. Dâryoush gets out of his van, comes over to me and, confronted with the woman's protestations, scolds me: 'What have you gone and done now?'

I don't say anything. He hands me the documents, and takes his doctor's card from his pocket to show to the recalcitrant woman.

'She suffers from serious depression,' he announces

confidently. 'I'm her doctor. She needs to go to *kharedj*, abroad, for treatment. I'm gone two minutes and she goes and gets attacked by someone like you.'

Despite Islamic restrictions he takes me by the hand (just like a doctor because – I think – they are allowed to give a dying woman the kiss of life) and drags me away from that dangerous place.

We go back up to the second floor. The staircase is clear now with just a few people coming down it. We head for the counter and have to wait our turn again.

'If I hadn't arrived just in time that shrew would have eaten you alive.'

I'm so frightened of seeing her again I keep turning round to look for her. All of a sudden an old woman in chador comes into the room, pronounces a few incomprehensible words and collapses on the floor. Dâryoush abandons me immediately to go and tend to her. When my turn comes I give my file to the officer, glancing anxiously over at Dâryoush. I need him more than ever now, him and the crafty words he's so good at whispering in policemen's ears. He's kneeling on the ground with his briefcase open, administering medicine to the woman.

'One last time . . .' she moans. 'Let me go to Karbala one last time . . .'

I don't have time to brandish the names Colonel Azardel and Lieutenant Mokhtarpour. The officer puts the file on to a pile of documents behind him, punctures my passport with a hole-puncher to invalidate it, stamps a piece of paper and hands me the perforated passport and the receipt. Then, without a word, he stands up, lowers the screen at his window and leaves.

The day is over. I go and join Dâryoush, who asks me to

sit down so the woman's head can rest in my lap. She doesn't stink of *shanbelileh*. The smell she gives off is of prayer stones, hushed libraries and dark staircases. I would like to stroke her forehead but resist the urge. When she lifts her head and sees the counter position is closed she starts to sob.

'I want to go to Karbala and die!' she wails.

I wasn't expecting that. I can feel tears rolling down my cheeks. Dâryoush manages rather awkwardly to sit the woman on a chair and asks me, 'Well? well? when will you have your passport?'

I tell him I gave the file to the officer.

'And?'

'And nothing.'

Dâryoush turns away from the woman towards me. Almost angry, he says, 'You shouldn't be crying for her but for your own future. She'll get to Karbala, there's no doubt about that. But you, you're a lost cause and now I've no idea when you'll get to France. I can't promise you anything.'

Apart from the old *chadori*, Dâryoush and myself, there's no one left in the office. We help the old woman downstairs while she goes on with her litany, 'I just want to go to Karbala one last time. To Karbala. To go to Karbala then die . . .'

I offer to see her home but she refuses. She'll wait her turn till tomorrow, right where she is.

'What do we do now?' I ask Dâryoush.

'I'm off to the morgue. But I'll call you this evening to tell you where we've got to.'

I thank him. He gets back into his van and leaves with his seat belt between his legs. It's half-past four. I've just spent seven hours with a pathologist from the morgue, a professor of criminology from the University of Law, a man who can't say no to a little local photographer.

I go back to my *ajans* and, finding the driver asleep, climb into the car hoping the sound of the door will wake him. In vain. I cough, then get out of the car and slam the door very loudly. He carries on sleeping.

'Excuse me! Excuse me! Please wake up!'

Nothing doing. I switch on my mobile and play a sequence of ringtones right by his ear. Now he sits up with a start. Success. I get back into the car and ask him to take me home. The car sets off but after barely five minutes he stops in front of a tiny shop with a sign saying SAND-WICHES FIRST, CINEMA NEXT. The driver gets out and explains, 'I'm sorry, madam. I must have a glass of tea. I don't want to seem rude but I haven't had anything to eat since this morning.'

I nod.

'Neither have you,' he adds. 'Come out and have a glass of tea with me. It won't do you any harm. It'll take us more than an hour to get into town so take pity on yourself. Don't say no to a little glass of tea.'

He's right. I get out of the car and together we go into the small teashop which smells of onions and kebabs. He orders omelettes and tea, offers me a table and goes and sits a little way away. I stand up and invite him to join me at my table. He refuses (an act of *tarof*) then accepts. The waiter brings tea, bread dotted with poppy seeds and fried eggs.

'*Befarmayin*, help yourself,' the driver says. 'It would be a sin to resist.'

Just then a lorry stops outside the shop. Two burly men get out: black jackets and open-neck white shirts. Around their necks they have *longs*, red and black cotton scarves, which they use to wipe the windscreen of their HGV. They ask to smoke a hookah. No problem.

My mobile rings and my husband's number in Paris comes up on the screen. I press the green button and listen to his ranting: 'Where on earth are you? I've been trying to get hold of you since this morning! I've called Mohtaram a thousand times and she keeps saying the same thing: telefon laterrr.'

He's right. 'Telefon laterrr' is the only piece of information Mohtaram can give foreigners who call me in Tehran. I explain quietly to my husband that I've spent the day at the passport office. The lorry drivers, my driver and the waiter are watching me and listening, dumbstruck.

'And? Did you get your passport in the end?' my husband asks.

What can I tell him? That I'm currently with my taxi driver sitting before a plate of fried eggs in a little teashop in southern Tehran, having spent the whole day at the passport office?

'Is your passport done then? When are you coming home?'

I keep quiet about the fact that my old passport is perforated and therefore unusable.

'Soon. I've just dropped off the renewal application. It's all done.'

'And when will you get it?'

'Now, that I don't know.'

The lorry drivers, my driver and the waiter are still staring at me. I'm suddenly afraid they're going to start brandishing visa forms under my nose.

'I can't talk now,' I tell my husband.

'Where are you, then?'

'Just about to eat fried eggs.'

'Don't forget we've been invited to Cannes, for the film festival. It's soon.'

The Cannes Film Festival seems a million miles away! I promise myself I'll remember the two lorry drivers, my *ajans* driver and the waiter as I climb up the red steps to the Palais des Festivals. I promise myself neither my spiky hair-pins nor the heels on my Bruno Frisoni shoes will make me forget these men met by chance around a plate of eggs and a hookah, and astonished to hear me suddenly speaking French into my mobile.

The driver pays the bill, which was probably very small. We get back into the car and an hour and a half later finally arrive outside my apartment block.

I ask him how much I owe him.

He replies by saying I'm his guest. Here we go, the *tarof* begins again. It's customary for taxi drivers to refuse payment and their customers to insist. After my third attempt I manage to secure a figure. I pay him and thank him for the fried eggs before getting out of the car.

In the hallway I can see Mr Eskandari getting to his feet.

'Where have you been all day?' he asks.

'At the passport office,' I tell him as I press the button for the lift.

He doesn't look surprised and makes the most of the opportunity to find out about the process.

'How long does a renewal take now?' he asks.

'More than a month.'

He still doesn't look surprised.

When I get into the apartment Mohtaram, who has just finished her prayers, warns me that my husband has called ten times. Then she launches into a long list of inaccurate names. Too tired to correct her, I throw myself on to my bed. I feel like calling Nargess and telling her about my adventure. But I resist the temptation. I'm really too tired. I can't do another thing.

Two hours later I'm back outside my aunt's apartment. Masserat opens the door with a scant smile. I kiss her, then Samira who seems even more glum than her sister-in-law. I can't see Hamid. He hasn't come to shake my hand. I imagine they must all resent me over the business with the mobile.

My daughter leaps into my arms, giggling. I can hear whispering and my heart suddenly melts in fear, worried for my uncle. I'm afraid something awful has happened to him but when I go into the living room, there he is lying on his bed. I'm reassured by the spectacle of his immobility. I look for my aunt and find her in her bedroom, huddled in an armchair with her head in her hands.

'Hamid's been arrested!' she says, sobbing (my aunt cries the whole time). 'He left this morning to take some time off then Dr Bashiri rang at about three o'clock to let us know Hamid had been arrested and he had opium on him.'

When I say I don't understand why she's crying she explains, 'Oh, no one can put themselves in my shoes! No one understands me! If Hamid . . .' She breaks off to wipe her face then carries on with a moan, 'if Hamid's not here who's going to wash your uncle and do his bedpan?'

'A nurse, another Hamid,' I say, handing her a box of tissues. 'I'll call Nargess right away and she'll find someone.'

'No one can replace Hamid,' she retorts, blowing her nose loudly. 'You don't seem to understand! How could I sleep in the next room to a *nareh khar*, a muscle-bound stranger?'

The conversation is closed. She's right. From her point of view, she's right. I ask her to describe how Hamid was arrested. She takes another tissue and blows her nose again.

'He was in Sar Asiab Malard,' she explains. 'The police did a raid and took everyone away. Dr Bashiri says everyone in that neighbourhood's a suspect in the eyes of the law, and even he could be arrested if he went there.'

I resist the urge to point out that if Dr Bashiri were there he wouldn't wander about with his pockets full of opium.

'Hamid called Dr Bashiri straight away,' my aunt goes on, 'and he, *may God grant him a long life*, went to the police station immediately to vouch for Hamid himself.'

'So are they releasing him?'

'No, they're going to keep him for a day or two. Before they let him go they're asking someone close to him to surrender title deeds on property as bail. Dr Bashiri, *how can I ever repay him*, is going back with the title deeds for his own apartment.'

My mobile rings. It's Nargess offering to take me to a show, an exhibition of railway lanterns. A collector's paradise! The Revolution turned every Iranian into a minor entrepreneur. When the Islamic Republic was established the leaders of the previous regime – those that hadn't fled the country – were imprisoned and all their assets confiscated. The wives, however, rose to the challenge: dispossessed of everything (cars, houses, drivers, maids and gardeners) they set about knitting and selling woollen waistcoats. Emboldened by early successes, some invested in sewing machines. They took on seamstresses – women of a lower class whose husbands were fighting at the front – and made children's clothes to sell in bulk to the malls in the Arab Emirates. I know one woman who raised enough money while her husband languished in prison to buy back her own car after two years and, after six years, to reclaim her confiscated house. When he was released her husband, who had once been the governor of a central province, returned to all the comforts of the 'old days' with the one difference that they had all been 'won back' by his wife.

Other less enterprising wives made do with taking on an anonymous tailor and getting him to copy the latest designs from Paris and Milan, arranging fashion shows – using their nieces and nieces' friends as models – and taking commissions from cousins and friends of cousins. When after a couple of seasons these budding 'fashion designers' (who had never so much as threaded a needle) went to Paris, they behaved like real professionals, severely criticising the crotch of Armani's trousers and the way Max Mara's sleeves were set in.

Others transformed their apartments into showrooms, filling them with merchandise from the Djomeh Bazaar – a cheap bric-à-brac sale on Fridays – and growing rich selling them at ten times the price to the diplomatic corps in the capital. Still others, who were more seasoned or more imaginative, introduced a cycle of themed shows.

That's exactly what Nargess is going to this evening, one of these shows, because a friend (it's always somebody's friend) has collected and put up for sale over a hundred railway lanterns – the sort that porters would once have swung on station platforms to guide the way for alighting passengers.

I turn down the invitation. I can't leave my aunt with a box of tissues on her lap. Shame about the lanterns.

'I'll come and pick you up after the show,' Nargess says. 'You're on my way.'

I know perfectly well I'm not on her way but, even with all the traffic jams, she'll make a big detour to see me.

To distract my aunt I tell her about my day spent with a pathologist who teaches criminology at the University of Law, a property developer searching for an eye, a woman who sells girls to Dubai, an old *chadori* who bribes the authorities with live chickens, and a driver *kolah makhmali* (with a finger cut short) with whom I shared the best fried eggs ever. She lets the box of tissues slip to the floor and eventually starts laughing.

Then all at once she asks, 'Do you think you could ask your doctor to go and pick Hamid up from the police station this evening?'

'No. That I can't do, I swear to you. I can't do it.'

My refusal sends her reeling back into the endless labyrinth of how much she needs Hamid but also into all his addictions, his failings, his laziness and weaknesses. She picks the box of tissues up again and hangs on to it. She daren't even tell her husband about the events of my day for fear that the sequence of misadventures could prove fatal to him. Perhaps for the first time in her life, she doesn't rush to tell him what she herself has just been told.

Meanwhile Hamid's wife and sister, Masserat and Samira, are arguing in the kitchen.

'If I ever get my hands on him,' Masserat announces, 'I'll cut him up into tiny pieces, *tikeh, tikeh.*'

'Shut up! It's because of you he got into all this. Before you were married he didn't even smoke cigarettes.'

'Oh, that's right, that's right. I married a saint and turned him into a waste of space.'

My aunt gets up to return to her post as commanding officer, and admonishes them forcefully, 'Be quiet now, the pair of you, that's enough! Be quiet or I'll get rid of both of you!'

Instant silence, even though this is an empty threat. When I walk past the kitchen a little later I see the three of them crying together.

Nargess calls: she's waiting for me in the car park. I go and say goodbye to my uncle who's snoozing in front of Euro News, which plays the same news pieces on a loop every thirty minutes. I say goodbye to the women, who are still in tears, put my scarf on and take my sleeping daughter in my arms.

Nargess opens the door to the car but I can't actually sit down because the front seat is so cluttered with lanterns. She struggles for a moment with their chains and, failing to unscramble them, suggests I sit in the back.

'I bought three,' she says, still battling with the chains.

'And what are you going to do with them?'

'If I can't hang them at home I'll put them in my mother's cellar. Do you know, Total's wife bought ten of them!'

Once I'm settled in the back of the car, I point out to Nargess that her scarf has slipped.

'It doesn't matter,' she says. 'I let my head get some fresh air at night.'

Nargess wears her white hair very short and is convinced that, behind a steering wheel, she can be mistaken for a man.

'Anyone seeing you on the rear seat will think I'm an *ajans* driver,' she adds rather proudly. 'One time last winter I gave a woman a lift and she went and sat in the back. I didn't really understand why but when we got to where she was going she asked how much she owed me. She actually thought I was one of those men who do a bit of taxi work on their way home from the office.'

Still, I suggest she lifts her scarf back up. I have no desire to end my day in front of a revolutionary committee along with all the girls arrested in the city's shopping centres, for failing to respect correct use of the veil. It can go as far as corporal punishment, as far as a whipping.

As she drives me home I tell her about my day. She's the only person I can tell everything without being reprimanded.

'Sometimes,' Nargess says, 'I suddenly start sweating as I'm going down a street.'

'Why?'

'Because that particular street reminds me of improbable meetings with people I didn't know but absolutely had to see to save our factory from bankruptcy. So you see Dâryoush and Yaft Abad . . .'

'Meanwhile you've saved your factory and I still don't have a passport.'

She's referring to a car parts factory which was confiscated from her family. I don't know exactly what sort of accessories they make there. Thanks to her tenacity – after more than ten years of different tactics, ruses and forms of leverage – Nargess has finally won. The factory has been given back.

We pass the Ecbatana studio. A light inside reveals my twelve chairs standing in a row, covered in jute. Well, that's one job done, at least.

'Don't let it bother you,' Nargess reassures me as we arrive. 'Either way you've saved a day or two. Don't lose track of your Dâryoush.'

'He was meant to ring me this evening.'

'Get inside and call him yourself.'

No, I can't call him at half-past midnight. The poor man worked so hard for me all day, he must be exhausted.

I'd rather let him sleep, but I don't tell Nargess this because, in my shoes, she wouldn't think twice about waking him.

When I get into the apartment with my daughter still asleep in my arms, I find Mohtaram performing the *namaz-e hadjat* prayer, in which a request is submitted to God.

When she has finished she doesn't speak to me. I don't say a word either. Sometimes it's right just to keep quiet. This evening, her God alone will know what it is she so wants. And I respect that.

I try to get to sleep by thinking about where Nargess could hang her lanterns.

All at once the telephone rings, startling me. It's Dâryoush.

'Nahal *djan*, did I wake you?' he asks.

'No,' I say automatically.

'Oh good. Well then, meet me at ten o'clock tomorrow morning outside the Firouzgar Hospital.'

'What for?'

'To get your passport, of course.'

I try to note down the time and place on one of my daughter's Dora the Explorer books.

'Get a photocopy of your receipt,' he adds, 'so you can give it to Colonel Azardel.'

'At the Firouzgar Hospital.'

'Yes. I'll be there, a bit before you. To dissect a body. A cousin of the colonel's, in fact. For now, goodnight and sleep well.'

I ring Nargess back straight away.

'You see, he did call you. You worried for nothing. Oh, by the way, we've got to go back to the record dealer we bought the Delkash boxed set from. They jump in places. I said we shouldn't trust that man.'

'He promised he'd exchange it if there was a problem.'

'Listen to this,' she says and holds the phone up. I can hear Delkash's hit *Ashofteh hali*, the one that always broke my mother's heart: 'To you I owe my fears and all my weakness, you with hair flowing over your shoulders. To you I owe my smile for this tumultuous life, you with your dark hair and dark, dark eyes.'

I remember my mother and her smile for this tumultuous life.

Tuesday

My daughter wakes me at eight o'clock by shining the beam of a torch in my eyes. Although apprehensive about this new day, I'm also drawn to Dâryoush's world as if by a strange magnetic force. I order an *ajans* with the secret hope of finding yesterday's *kolah makhmali* again and perhaps having lunch with him after the Firouzgar Hospital in a cheap and cheerful *tchelo kababi*.

When the *ajans* arrives it's not the same driver. Today's could be a bank clerk . . . I mean he really could be: under a formal grey jacket he's wearing a shirt but no tie (ties are universally frowned upon by Islam, hence the Mao-style collarless shirts worn by Iranian officials at the UN and international summits). Still, I tell him where we're going with a degree of self-assurance. This confidence is based on the fact that the Firouzgar Hospital was founded by a friend's grandfather and I, therefore, feel the place can't be completely hostile towards me.

I find comfort where I can.

The man chooses the worst, the slowest, the most congested motorway to get there. I want to speak out but don't know the name of the one that would be free-flowing, hesitating – inside my head – between the names of various generals who died in the war. In the end I give up on the idea of directing him. I'll probably be late. Never mind.

The car's sound system blares the voice of a very young girl ardently declaiming love poems and complaining that she's been betrayed and abandoned. I ask the driver, cautiously, whether it's a national radio station or a CD. I don't want to give the impression I live abroad, it would instantly double the price of the trip.

'It's a CD,' he tells me. 'I buy everything she does.'

I'm lost. I was hoping the song was on the radio so I might dare ask him to switch it off. But this is a CD, my driver's personal choice, so I'm condemned to listen right to the bitter end. Now the girl's complaining (and it's hardly original) that she's been replaced by someone else in her lover's fickle heart. It gives me goose pimples. How can women be banned from singing when a child (eleven, twelve years old?) can spout impassioned words in public? I tell myself it must have been recorded in Los Angeles by the Iranian diaspora. Via satellite they inundate Iran with music clips featuring young Iranian girls with curvaceous buttocks and augmented breasts singing the age-old refrains of separation in Persian. They also give us so-called scientific programmes in which a 'psychoanalyst' live on air answers questions from neurotic fellow-countrymen bemoaning their decision to stay in Iran. Alongside these are the almost daily 'political debates' which have been rehashing a countdown of the Islamic Republic's existence for nearly thirty years.

The driver hands me the CD case. I read the singer's name, Maryam Heydarian, above a picture of a young woman in dark glasses.

'But how old is this singer?' I ask.

'Don't you know her?'

'No.'

He used the respectful you-form which is often the case in *ajans* where people tend to keep a certain distance.

'How can you not know her? The whole of Iran's talking about her. She's blind. She must be about twenty-two or three. But she's still got the voice of a child.'

I've been found out. He now knows I don't live in Iran. The fare has instantly doubled, perhaps tripled.

The still-childish voice carries on weeping its sorry fate, and I carry on finding it unbearable and missing the silence of yesteday's *kolah makhmali*.

We finally reach the Firouzgar Hospital a quarter of an hour late. I call Dâryoush and he asks me to get out of the taxi and wait a few minutes by the flower stall. I get out, delighted to escape the syrupy simpering of that young blind girl with her doll-like voice. I wait on the pavement for a quarter of an hour, then half an hour. The hospital doorman is starting to worry about me hanging about. Who am I? What am I doing here at eleven o'clock in the morning? I pre-empt him and explain that I'm an acquaintance of Dr Askarnia and am waiting for him. He seems satisfied with this and moves away while I go back to walking up and down the pavement.

A man walks past and mutters quickly out of the corner of his mouth, 'D'you fuck?'

This is the most direct pick-up line in Iran. The most effective? Hmm . . .

Without replying, without even a shrug of my shoulders, I go back to the car and the infantile whingeing of the blind singer who still hasn't finished being dumped. I sit back down on the rear seat. A quarter of an hour later

I call Dâryoush again. No connection. I get out of the car, a home-grown Peykan, and go over to the gates of the hospital where I dial Dâryoush's number once more. This time he answers. He even pops his head out of a window on the second floor, waves his scalpel and cries, 'Don't move, I've nearly finished! I've just got the intestine to do! Just the intestine,' he reiterates, swiping the scalpel through the air.

I look away. The man who propositioned me so bluntly is on the pavement opposite, still waiting for my answer. I go over to the flower stall and – very, very slowly – choose two pots of jasmine. I pay and the florist takes the pots over to the Peykan. I follow him closely, afraid of being accosted again by the man waiting on the other pavement.

My mobile rings: it's Dâryoush.

'*Ey baba*, where are you?' he asks. 'I did ask you to wait by the flower stall, didn't I?'

I turn round and there he is, standing in front of some pots of geraniums, surrounded by five strapping men, including Colonel Azardel. I explain that I'm on the other side of the street, just five metres away. When he spots me he says quietly, 'Don't forget to give your condolences to the colonel.'

I certainly won't. Having gone over and greeted the colonel, I add, 'I hope this will be your last bereavement.'

He thanks me with a nod, looks at Dâryoush who whispers something in his ear, and asks me for the receipt from yesterday. I take it from my bag. Then he asks for my mobile number, which I give him, despite screams from my little voice which I instantly silence. The colonel jots down my number above the Koranic script at the top of a death certificate.

I give Dâryoush a questioning look.

'You needn't worry now,' he says. 'In spite of everything he's going through at the moment, the colonel will personally take care of your passport.'

I know I shouldn't do this and ought to respect his recent bereavement, but I want to know more.

'When will it be ready?' I ask Dâryoush.

'A week at the latest. I'll call you. Don't worry, it's all under control.'

I thank the colonel, Dâryoush and the other men, and get back into the car. I close my eyes – even the blind woman's puerile voice doesn't bother me now.

When we arrive outside my building the *tarof* begins with the driver.

'How much do I owe you?'

'Be my guest, this once.'

I open my purse and take a few notes out.

'Thank you very much. How much is it?'

He picks up a notebook, puts on his glasses and studies a series of tables full of figures.

'Ten thousands *tomans*,' he concludes.

I settle up without complaining and without pointing out that for a trip like that he should only have taken six thousand.

Inside I find Mr Eskandari in the hall with my twelve chairs arranged in two rows.

'The photographers came earlier,' he announces.

'Why didn't they go up?'

'There was no one in. Mrs Mohtaram left in a terrible rush and took the little one with her.'

'But why was she in such a rush?'

'I don't know.'

I leave the chairs in the hall and call my aunt straight

away. Please say nothing's happened to my uncle. Luckily she answers herself, sparing me my daily enumeration of every member of Mohtaram's family. My aunt's voice doesn't betray traces of any new disaster.

'Before they released Hamid,' she tells me, 'they wanted to speak to his parents. Mohtaram came over, left Kiara here and then went to the police station with Dr Bashiri, *may God increase his standing and honour tenfold.*'

I take this opportunity to reassure my aunt about my new passport, regurgitating what Dâryoush said word for word: 'Colonel Azardel is personally taking care of my application.'

She seems satisfied. A colonel, now that's reassuring.

'One last thing,' she adds. 'Mr Sabeti is going to come and see you later.'

'Why?'

'Because Kiara can't get any children's channels any more.'

Mr Sabeti is our satellite dish man. In Iran the whole question of satellite dishes involves a subtle game of cat and mouse between the authorities and millions of users. Officially, everything is banned but in practice every little apartment block has five or six dishes judiciously hidden in corners and on roofs. How vigilant the Revolutionary Guards are depends directly on Iran's international relations. Since the whole nuclear weapons incident, there have been many more checks and a lot of people have started taking their dishes down, with the idea of putting them back up when things are going better, stowing them carefully in their original packaging (in Iran everyone keeps original packaging. In the bazaar I've even seen a whole aisle dedicated to selling it).

I know that in a few days my aunt will hide her dish too,

hoping it's only temporarily. In the meantime I take the risk of keeping mine up and even – the cheek of it! – program it to children's channels. Technicians delight in using the English word upgrade to describe this operation, and Mr Sabeti's sentences are littered with at least three *upgrades*, producing something along these lines: 'First I'll have to *upgrade* your French channels, madam. And that *upgrade* alone will take a couple of hours. Then if you'd like me to *upgrade* the other channels you'll have to wait till tomorrow. Because I have to go to your aunt and *upgrade* her Euro News.'

A deformed version of Mr Sabeti's face appears on the videophone. He is about forty, completely clean shaven and fragrant with aftershave. His work, which he performs in total secrecy, requires him to look if not actually elegant, at least presentable. I prepare to be bombarded with *upgrades* as he comes in with his laptop, briefcase and several metres of different coloured cables. He knows he need not take his shoes off in my house, and heads straight for the library where the television is. He switches it on, sits on the sofa, pores over his laptop and starts the familiar upgrading operation.

I leave him on his own while he calls a colleague.

'To upgrade the Piwi channel . . . It is Piwi your daughter watches, madam, isn't it?' he asks me.

'Yes?'

'How do I access that?'

'Piwi or Tiji or Channel J,' I call from the living room. 'It doesn't matter much but do please get France 2 and France 3, and Arte . . . Oh, and also leave me the Islamic Republic channels, don't get rid of them.'

'You must be the only customer who doesn't ask me to

get rid of the official channels and to upgrade obscure French channels instead of things from Los Angeles. What's so great about Arte? I tried to watch it once and when we were trying to eat they put on a programme about polio! Do you think we need that in Iran?'

I don't say anything but let him get on with it. The telephone rings and it's my cousin, the wine expert. She needs to renew her passport and has just heard from my aunt that I've managed to avoid the twenty-four-hour queue and the new one-month waiting time.

'Could you put me in touch with the guy who set this up for you?'

'It hasn't happened yet. It's all in the air. I don't even know if I'll actually get my passport.'

'Well, if you don't want to tell me who he is . . .'

'Of course I will! Only I hardly know him. What if he turns out to be incompetent, full of hot air . . . Wait till I've got my passport. Then I'll tell you how to get in touch with him.'

She hangs up, apparently annoyed.

Mr Sabeti coughs before coming into the living room where I'm sitting. It's customary in traditional families for *na mahrams* (people who are not family members) to announce themselves with a little cough or other sound.

'Madam, I'm taking this opportunity when *khanoum* Mohtaram's not here to let you know it would be a good idea to block porn channels. You know that section of society has been deprived of so much for so long that exposure to images like that can send them completely off the rails.'

I'd rather not tell him Mohtaram herself claims that where she comes from in Kashmar in eastern Iran people watch porn films for hours on end. In fact when she herself was setting off on a trip to Mecca (financed by me after I'd expressed my longing for a child), the day before she left a young cousin of hers turned up on her doorstep with a ten dollar bill and the address of a lingerie boutique not far from Kaaba.

'Keep an eye out for it,' the girl told her. 'Just as you come out of the "House of God" turn to your left a bit and you'll see the fuchsia-coloured sign for the lingerie shop.'

Mohtaram only wanted to go to Mecca to see God, or at least his faithful followers.

'Go inside,' the young cousin went on. 'All the different designs are displayed on hangers so you don't even need to worry about the language barrier. You won't have to ask for anything. Get me the G-string with an opening at the front shaped like a heart. It's easy. Get me two of them, one in red, one in leopardskin. OK?'

Mohtaram, who only wanted to buy pilgrim's rosaries and holy water, still took the ten dollars and reassured her cousin that she really would come home from Mecca with two G-strings in her suitcase, one red, the other leopardskin, with a heart-shaped opening at the front.

But she didn't have the nerve. When she got home, when the young G-string requester came to see her, Mohtaram handed back the ten dollars along with a pocket-sized Koran as a souvenir. Spitting with rage, the young woman snatched the ten dollars saying there wasn't much point going to Mecca if you didn't bring anything interesting back, and stalked out without even drinking her glass of tea.

When I asked Mohtaram who this flighty cousin was planning to wear the G-string for, she said, 'For her husband, obviously.'

'What does her husband do?'

'He's a dustman.'

Despite Mohtaram's knowledge of pornographic material (which she claims is so common where she comes from), I agree with Mr Sabeti's initiative and tell him he can block the porn channels. It has to be said these films give a peculiar image of the West, a false image of course and even an extravagant one: all any woman wants is to throw herself at every passing man. But for a great many simple-minded people this image passes for the truth. It results in widespread and permanent frustration, provoking depths of solitary perversion which I daren't even imagine . . . but also aggravates the negation of Iranian women. And the same is true of other Islamic countries.

'If I'm going to block them,' the clean-shaven engineer goes on, 'I'll need you there because sometimes when you block a channel you lose others at the same time. No one knows why.'

My little voice goes berserk (too risky! it's too risky!) and recommends abandoning the operation which would necessitate sitting on the sofa in the library watching porn channels with Mr Sabeti. Yet again I don't listen to my little voice. I sit down on the sofa, some way away from the engineer, granted, to protect myself from intoxicating wafts of his eau de cologne. Mr Sabeti, remote in hand, zaps energetically, identifies a porn channel, stays on it for a moment (to be absolutely sure it really is one), presses a few buttons to block the system and steams on to the next one, without a word.

My little voice tries to get me to stand up and leave the room. But I stay, out of idleness or because I have thought it through. After all, images are Mr Sabeti's profession. Sitting next to him looking at the vagina and anus of a moaning blonde, penetrated simultaneously and in close-up by two huge black penises is no more compromising, I tell myself, than trying on a pair of trousers for a tailor.

I try to convince myself, although I don't entirely succeed.

The videophone rings again. I abandon Mr Sabeti and the hard-working porn stars. The face on the screen doesn't mean anything to me so I switch on the intercom and ask, 'Who is it?'

Despite the bad quality of the picture, I can now make out a hand pushing back some hair and, at the same time, I hear a voice saying, '*Salam*, it's Morad. I'm here, downstairs. Shall I bring the chairs up?'

That's all I need – him and the twelve chairs. I suggest he brings them up four at a time in the lift.

I wonder how delivery men and visitors conspire to turn up at the same time, precisely when Mohtaram is out. I'll have to offer them tea and I've never known how to make the stuff to everybody's individual liking. Some have it in a cup, others in small narrow *kamar barik* glasses. Still others refuse to drink tea unless it's served in large Turkish-style glasses and has infused for a long time. As for the colour, it has to be dark for some and pale for others. If you make the mistake of serving weak tea to an adherent of the strong variety, he'll reject it and compare it to *ab-e zipo*, which is soup. By the same token, if you offer very dark tea to someone who likes it weak, he won't touch it but will look away with a, 'don't bring that drug addict's stew near me'.

There are infinite permutations of refusal. Oh, the embarrassment if you inadvertently serve lukewarm strong tea in a *kamar barik* to someone who loves light-coloured scalding hot tea in a tall Turkish glass. So what to do? To

sidestep the diverse and often contradictory requirements
of my guests, I've decided to give everyone coffee.
Mohtaram is quick to tell me that offering the very good
coffee I bring from Paris to decorators, carpenters, engineers and every sort of workman who does an odd job in
my apartment is quite simply a waste, but I don't set any
store by her opinion. When I'm on my own and have
guests to look after, coffee comes to my rescue.

Morad comes in with four chairs under his arms. I
would like to shake his hand so he puts down the chairs
and returns the greeting. He wants to take his shoes off but
I remind him he can keep them on here. Anyway, he has
to go back down to get the other eight chairs, which will
take two more trips. He picks the first four chairs back up,
carries them into the dining room and asks, 'You did see
Dr Askarnia, didn't you?'

In a few words I tell him how very helpful Dr Askarnia
was and that he did everything in his power for me. The
moans of some ecstatic blonde reach us from the library. I
hurriedly explain that an engineer is upgrading (I use the
English word although I don't really know what it means) my
satellite dish. Morad runs his hand through his hair but makes
no comment before going out to get more of the chairs.

I go into the kitchen, hastily make some coffee and
invite Mr Sabeti to come into the living room. He gives a
little cough before entering the room then, when he smells
the coffee, exclaims, '*Bah, bah*, you're the only person who
makes such good coffee. Doing upgrades under these conditions isn't work at all, it's a luxury!'

Just then Morad comes back with four more chairs
under his arms. The two men greet each other with recip-
rocal mistrust. It's obvious neither of them sees the other's
presence here in a good light. Why? I wonder.

'I'll go up and hide your satellite dish,' Mr Sabeti says.
'Where?'

'On the terrace that belongs to the lady on the top floor. You know, behind those big pots of *nazri*, ritual offerings.'

'But isn't it dangerous for my neighbour to "accommodate" my dish?'

'No,' he assures me. 'Oh no, she can take it. She isn't afraid of anything. Believe me, if everyone was like her we wouldn't be in the state we're in.'

He drains his coffee and, as he gets to his feet, adds, '*Ba edjazeh*, with your permission.'

He goes out and Morad waits for the doors to the lift to close before speaking.

'Are you paying that man to upgrade your channels?'

'Yes, Mr Sabeti is hired by the managing agent for this building.'

This is a lie: Mr Sabeti works completely illegally. Morad, who has probably guessed this, pushes his point. 'How much are you giving him for this upgrade?'

'Fifty thousand *tomans*,' I announce, halving the real figure.

'That much? Tell me, do Hassan and I look handicapped or something for you to feel you have to use people like him?'

'Mr Sabeti performs his duties competently and honestly.'

'Is that honesty, then? Twiddling away on his laptop, watching those – excuse me – X-rated channels with a woman of your standing, happily sipping the best coffee in Tehran and charging that sort of price? Is that honesty?'

My little voice warns me not to be sidetracked, I really

must forget the satellite dish and chairs, and concentrate on my passport. For once I listen to it and ask, 'Would you say I should call Dr Askarnia now or not?'

He goes over to the four chairs and, as if he hasn't heard my question, points to them proudly, saying, 'Just look at that work! Your chairs re-covered and delivered within forty-eight hours!'

I thank him (at the moment I'm not really interested in the chairs) and go back to my main concern.

'If you were me would you call Dr Askarnia or not?' I ask.

Morad glances at Mr Sabeti's empty cup.

'If I were you, do you know what I'd do? I throw that so-called engineer out. And right away!'

'So I shouldn't be worried about my passport then?'

He clears his hair off his forehead with what he thinks is an elegant gesture, and declares with great confidence, 'The doctor is like a brother to me.'

I feel reassured. For now I don't need to call Dâryoush, which is what Nargess would definitely be suggesting. I pour Morad a cup of coffee and drink a glass of sugar water (needs must with low blood pressure) to prepare myself for the usual *tarof* session which precedes every form of payment.

'*Agha* Morad,' I say in a curt, almost unfriendly voice, 'would you be so kind as to let me know straight out, with no preamble, how much I owe you for the chairs.'

To my considerable astonishment he asks, 'Including delivery?'

'Including delivery.'

'Eighty thousand *tomans*.'

It's a victory. I've just saved half an hour. I pay without quibbling. Before he leaves I even run and get two tins of coffee and offer them to him as a thank-you for putting me in touch with Dâryoush.

'One each for your wife and Hassan's,' I tell him.

He takes them and says he's going to fetch the last four chairs. As he leaves, Mr Sabeti, who is coming back down from the roof, emerges from the lift. His eyes immediately home in on the two tins of coffee Morad is holding.

'I've camouflaged the dish,' he tells me, 'so even a *djen*, a winged genie, wouldn't be able to find it.'

He comes in, inspects the chairs contemptuously and adds, 'So now people cover chairs with sacking and call it upholstery?' (although Morad can't hear him because he's already in the lift).

'*Agha* Morad is a photographer, you know. He's been kind enough to deliver them for me.'

I'd rather not mention the two wives who sew for a living. Who knows where that might end up? Mr Sabeti shrugs and prepares to go. I leave him for a moment and come back with another tin of coffee.

'A little something for you. Here. Now wherever you are you'll just have to have some of this and your work will instantly become a pleasure. Or even a luxury, as you called it.'

That is when Morad comes back, carrying the last four chairs. He sees the tin of coffee I've just given the engineer and which the latter is making no attempt to conceal – quite the opposite: he's holding it close to his chest like a trophy. This gift does little to please the photographer, I can see that. Meanwhile, Mr Sabeti can't disguise his contempt for the upholstery work.

Gesturing towards the chairs, he tells me, 'Just so you know, I didn't say that to get special treatment.'

'It's just a little something,' I insist, pointing at the coffee. 'Just a souvenir.'

'What did Mr Engineer here say about the chairs?' asks Morad.

'Nothing, nothing, he didn't say anything.'

I haven't the strength for this. Can't they both just go now?

And they do. Maybe they'll carry on with their conversation in the lift. It doesn't bother me.

I head for my bed. My little voice warns me that I haven't even looked at the chairs. I leave it to its doubts, I'm too tired to be upset.

'Eighty thousand *tomans* for shoddy work! Come on!' my little voice carries on muttering.

I go back into the living room and inspect two or three chairs. Mr Sabeti was right: the results aren't very satisfactory. The job has been done quickly and badly. But I console myself with the thought that those eighty thousand *tomans* saved me queuing for forty-eight hours and the nervous exhaustion that would have entailed.

I go to sleep trying, once again, to find a home for the railway lanterns in Nargess's apartment. The telephone rings: it's my husband.

'So, how's your passport going?'

'I met the big cheese today, the boss man. He told me it would take a week.'

'I don't understand. I tell you, I just don't understand what's going on over there. So you won't be back for Cannes?'

'I'm afraid I probably won't. But I hope I'll be back in time for Venice.'

'But Venice is at the beginning of September, and we haven't been invited anyway!'

I don't know what to tell him. I was trying to make a joke. I reassure him as best I can, try to calm him down.

How can I explain all my convoluted efforts over the telephone?

A little later I get a call from Nargess. She would like us to go and have dinner in a Japanese restaurant. No, I can't see myself sitting in the lotus position eating sashimi with my scarf tied under my chin. I say she should come and eat with me instead. We'll order sandwiches from Bix, the fashionable take-out place, and we'll watch *Mar adentro* on DVD.

And suddenly there she is on my bed. I must have slept for a quarter of an hour. Nargess knows everyone in Tehran, she can get into any building without being interrogated by the caretaker. She can be in a lift anywhere and, after only a few seconds, will know the name of the stranger in there with her. She'll even know how many mistresses he has and how wealthy he is. It goes something like this: 'Do you know, in the Shah's day, that man owned every single factory producing cooking oil. Now he works with mullahs. His wife's seeing a Belgian diplomat and he has a nice line in twenty year old girls. He's just bought a one thousand square metre, three-storey apartment with a swimming pool on the roof.'

Nargess takes the Bix menu from her bag. It's in English and we have to exploit all our linguistic abilities to decipher the list of sandwiches. After a certain amount of hesitation, we settle for two California Clubs and place our order. While we wait I give Nargess a brief summary of my day. But, before anything else, she insists on checking the braid on the chairs.

'So do you think my passport's going to be OK?' I ask as she glues her face to the upholstery on one of the seats.

'You've got to call Dâryoush every day,' she tells me. 'Several times a day, even,' she adds and then, not waiting for my reply, goes straight on with, 'What on earth have they done here? I could have done better myself! They've stuck the braiding on with Uhu!'

She grabs one end of the braid and exclaims, 'Look, I'm only just touching it and it's coming away! I'm not even pulling! Eighty thousand *tomans* for that!'

She is probably right, but I've got other things on my mind.

The delivery man arrives soon after that. Then a great war breaks out between Nargess and myself over paying for the sandwiches. My argument strikes me as incontrovertible: 'You're in my house!'

'All right.'

She agrees to be my guest. I pay the twenty thousand *tomans* and we unwrap our sandwiches: two tiny slices of bread with four cherry tomatoes and two transparent slivers of 'chicken ham' – given that eating pork is forbidden by Islam. We swallow them in one mouthful in the corridor, before we get to the library.

I put the DVD of *Mar adentro* on but before the film starts Nargess declares, 'We were had with those sandwiches, that's for sure. But as for the chairs, you can't accept them. Call your photographers straight away so I can have a word with them.'

The titles are starting.

'*Badan, badan*, later,' I say.

Nargess closes her eyes after just five minutes. They won't open again until the last frame. An hour and a half of peace. After that my aunt calls to let me know Mohtaram and Kiara are on their way home. She asks what we are doing, and I avoid telling her I've just watched a film about a handicapped man who can't get out of bed and whose only hope is that someone will help him die.

Nargess leaves and Mohtaram and Kiara come home. I take my daughter to bed with me, ignoring paediatricians' advice that children should be encouraged to sleep alone.

Badan, badan, later, later.

And I go to sleep without finding anywhere for Nargess's lanterns.

Wednesday

This morning, freed from concerns about my passport, I ask a very dear friend, an erudite French-speaker who has translated Balzac (amongst others), to come with me to a *passaj*, a shopping centre.

The clothes that young Iranian women wear in these places require particular attention. And are very revealing. Given that the veil is compulsory, girls invest all their artistry and skill in finding some way of showing as much hair as possible. To counter the inertia of that simple square of fabric, they have invented a complete scaffolding arrangement – using combs and slides – to create a mane of raised hair, preferably blonde, which is allowed to escape from the scarf. Their eyes and eyebrows constantly change colour and shape. At the moment the tendency is to have very dark eyes (the people importing different coloured contact lenses must have gone bankrupt) and eyebrows tattooed on in the shape of a pointed Chinese hat. Their fringes tumble down from the scaffolding, providing a fan of colours from fuchsia through to platinum blonde, while designer sunglasses perched on top of their heads hide the alleged scarf. The wings of their noses have been refined by surgery so many times as to be virtually invisible. Their mouths, pumped outrageously with silicon, stick out further than their noses. Their ears are invariably decked out with big hoop earrings and MP3 player earphones. They wear stretch leggings, platform-heel sandals which display their artfully decorated toenails, and jackets two sizes too small which barely cover their buttocks. The younger and prettier they are, the shorter and tighter their jackets have to be, even though they frequently get arrested for being dressed like this.

Far from being a superficial phenomenon, fashion in this country is a political attitude. These girls are almost all tall and slim, unlike their mothers who are short and fat. They all carry fake Vuitton, Gucci or Prada in their brightly manicured hands – oh, and a mobile phone which is indispensable. Some have two, one in each hand. The air is asphyxiated by their perfume. Thirty years of Islamic power have failed to impose a female ideal on them: a dark, hidden woman covered with a black chador and wearing boring flat shoes, saving any coquettishness she may have for the ritual Thursday evening marital union.

What do we see of Iranian women in the West? Either this grim, gloomy, even forbidding image which seems to negate itself but will, on command, burn the odd American flag. Or a rich Botoxed specimen with gleaming skin and an Hermès scarf, driving her own Mercedes with her golf clubs on the back seat.

Between these two extremes, where is Iran?

In recent years young men, quite safe from the trials and imprisonment which constantly threaten women (a sixteen-year-old girl was recently hanged for 'adultery' when she wasn't even married), have adopted female aesthetics.

Boys in Tehran, at least those who frequent the *passajs*, all have surgically improved noses, plucked eyebrows, manicured nails and long, slicked-back hair. This too is a far cry from the image of the practising Muslim.

We pass a coffee shop heaving with young couples who love each other but are not allowed to kiss, fondle or hold hands. Further along is a café for lesbians where most of the tables are taken by women. Here I see one customer surreptitiously pushing back her friend's scarf and kissing her earlobe.

As usual I'm wearing trousers and a roomy tunic from Pleats, sheltered from prying eyes. Davar, my translator friend, and I go into a luxury leather goods shop which specialises in forgeries. The salesgirl – the wings of her nose are so non-existent that you can only see her nostrils, two gaping holes in the middle of her face – has impossibly long white fingers adorned with fake Bulgari rings. Unlike other more chaotic shops, the shelves here display only a few designs of bags (Vuitton, Gucci, Prada), belts (Dolce & Gabbana, Burberry) and glasses (Dior and Chanel). The floor is in black marble and the furniture in tobacco brown leather.

The salesgirl – who must have been specially taught how to look down on customers – has delineated a field of vision for herself in which we do not feature. In other words, she doesn't see us. And a good thing too. I take advantage of this to study the prices which are skilfully hidden in inside pockets, and are five times higher than anywhere else. I point to a backpack-style Vuitton bag and ask her how much it is. She inhales a lungful of (conditioned) air, which seems to narrow the wings of her nose still further, and deigns to reply in Persian tinged with an American accent, 'Two hundred and fifty thousand *tomans*.'

When I venture to inform her that the same bag is being sold in the shop opposite for fifty thousand *tomans* she excludes me from her field of vision once more.

'The shop opposite gets its stock from Turkey while we . . .' she begins, then draws in another lungful of air before finishing her sentence, 'we get ours from Italy.'

Next she glances quickly at my clothes and, probably judging them unworthy of her boutique and even of the one opposite which does its buying in Turkey, she adds, 'Go down to the floor below and you'll find the cheaper ones made in Iran.'

It's high time I returned some of her disdain. Before leaving I linger a little longer, trying out oversized glasses, and then out of the blue I ask Davar how he's getting on with his translation of *La Peau de chagrin*. Not thinking for a moment that this is one of my strategies, he immediately replies, 'I'm having trouble with the sentence "*Mon amour veut des échelles de soie escaladées en silence, par une nuit d'hiver.*"'

The effect of this sentence, spoken in French, is to put the salesgirl back in her place. I put the enormous glasses down on her desk, attaching no importance to them at all, and carry on in French, 'And tell me Davar, what will you be translating once you've finished *La Peau de chagrin*?'

As we leave I thank the salesgirl through pinched lips, without turning to look at her. It's my turn now – with all my French speaking and Balzac reading – to eclipse her from my horizons. She no longer exists.

'*Le Médecin de campagne,*' replies Davar, who hasn't noticed our subterranean confrontation.

We go into the shop opposite, the one that buys its fakes in Turkey, and the salesman in here is welcoming. He calls Davar *mohandess* which means 'engineer'. If my friend were wearing a tie he would call him 'doctor' because since the Revolution the only people who have kept their ties are doctors. So anyone wearing a tie is referred to with the title 'doctor' even if he's a lawyer, or unemployed. *Mohandess* is used for men who look sophisticated: linen trousers, Lacoste polo shirt and Ray-Ban glasses. That is in fact more or less what Davar is wearing. On top of this he adopts a particular diction, bearing and professorial stance that mean no one readily contradicts him.

Here, like everywhere else, the be-turbaned portrait of the Supreme Guide is given pride of place. A stereo plays Iranian pop music recorded in Los Angeles. The shelves are laden with bags, shoes, belts and wallets. Vuitton and Gucci catalogues are laid out on a coffee table. I dig out the same backpack and show it to Davar. True enough, it's a third the price.

All of a sudden a group of women run through the mall. The salesgirl opposite, the one whose forgeries are made in Italy, nervously lowers the shutters to her shop. In a flash our salesman replaces the Vuitton catalogues with a pile of *Keyhan* (a conservative daily paper), switches off the music, turns on the official radio and turns round the Louis Vuitton sign behind which he has already stuck a picture of Kaaba.

'It's the vice squad. They're here. I hope they won't cause too much damage.'

We go over to the window.

'Please sit down,' he advises me.

I do as I'm told.

The women hurtle past, Revolutionary Guards veiled in black from head to foot. One of them lunges into the boutique we're in. The salesman says hello. She doesn't answer but inspects what I'm wearing without a word.

'There we are! They've just arrested four girls,' says Davar, standing in the doorway.

These raids in shopping centres, restaurants, public parks, and even private apartments, are part of daily life for Iranians. Those in power are mostly targeting the young but it's not unheard of for older people to be arrested, particularly for alcohol consumption.

For thirty years now the Armenian minority (the only community, with the exception of embassies, permitted to drink alcohol in private) has been supplying most of Iran with spirits. Every family has its own Armenian, and some have better reputations than others. My aunt's delivers at any time of day or night, Nargess's is renowned for his vodka, and Davar's also sometimes brings boar meat which is forbidden because it's effectively pork.

Since the Islamic Republic was instituted, alcohol consumption has been officially prohibited. But people still drink. According to one anecdote, before the Revolution Iranians prayed at home and drank out in the open whereas after the Revolution they took to drinking at home and praying at work (to demonstrate their faith) and in the street in large gatherings.

Apart from the Armenians, whose merchandise is smuggled into ports in southern Iran, middle-aged housewives have relinquished jam-making and *torshis* recipes in favour of making wine. In the bazaar once I watched with my own eyes as a woman bought two hundred kilos of grapes: she clearly wasn't planning to eat them with her family. Now every household, or nearly, makes its own wine. I've never known why but the French have taken the upper hand over everyone else in this homespun wine-making. As an example, guests of an architect who studied at the Beaux-Arts in Paris taste his wine as if it were a Château

Cheval Blanc, but would scorn the brew of a contemporary of his with a lowly degree from some university in Texas – sometimes even spitting it out.

There's no point saying it's all bad. In this wine-producing competition, there are very few who have actual wine bottles. Take the Paris architect: he had to ferret out countless bottles in the antique shops round Manoutchehri and Djomeh Bazaar. And when he brings wine to one of my friends' houses, he never fails to ask for the bottle back, like an old granny hanging on to her jam jars.

The Texan architect, on the other hand, serves his wine in squash bottles. I've even seen (though never drunk) wine in Coke bottles. A French-speaking cousin of mine, who has pronounced herself a wine connoisseur, always starts by asking for a large wine glass with a stem. She pours wine into it, commenting on the colour in the process, then swirls the glass slowly in her hand, puts her redesigned nose into it, moistens her gums, keeps the wine in her mouth for a moment with half-closed eyes, and eventually – watched in fascination by everyone else – delivers her peremptory and definitive opinion. Every time she goes to Paris she makes a point of learning by heart the vintage and price of a few famous wines so she can bewitch her entourage (and these are people who serve wine in Coke bottles) by quoting endless lists of enchanting mythical names such as Romanée-Conti 1929 or Mouton-Rothschild 1982, oh, if you only knew . . .

Tehranians particularly like frequenting foreign embassies because they can drink as much as they like there. The wine served isn't particularly good but it is better than anything produced locally, such as the Paris architect's offerings. In the early days of the Islamic Revolution foreign embassies even set up tasting competitions. The French regularly won the red wine competition with their 'Château de Neauphle' – a nod to Neauphle-le-Château, the village in Yvelines where Ayatollah Khomeyni settled in exile. But the Germans, who had probably bribed the Italians (at least that was what the French ambassador thought) came out on top for white wine.

The French ambassador himself told me that when the grapes were brought to the embassy after the harvest, everyone employed there, men and women, regardless of rank, went down to the cellars to tread the grapes with their bare feet. One day, right in the middle of the American hostage crisis, a group of inspectors from the French Foreign Office made a surprise visit to check over security systems in embassies believed to be at risk. In their report they made a point of commenting on the pitiful state of the shredder intended for reducing confidential documents to confetti. No one on the embassy staff admitted that the machine was mostly used for crushing grapes, which had caused it considerable damage.

Another ban: a single lock of dyed hair peeping out beneath a scarf can send a woman to prison. Those arrested for contravening this law are taken before a committee of revolutionary administrators and, after mortifying interrogations, are kept in for two or three days without sleep, food or contact with the outside world. At the end of this period the revolutionary commandos contact the detainee's parents or family and ask for the title deeds to property as bail. Depending on the nature of the crime (obvious make-up, ankles showing, hair visible, alcohol on breath) they then demand the relevant sum of money. Anyone who refuses to pay is condemned to flogging. One of my friends, who has never accepted these arbitrary rulings, once refused to pay her fine and was given one

hundred lashes of the whip. She had set off to go to the
bookshop but came home after two days' absence with her
books in her hand and blood all over her back.

The salesman opens a drawer and takes out a press cutting
with a photograph of the Commander-in-Chief of
Tehran's armed forces posing in front of a blackboard with
the following instructions:

- Bright lipstick? > Do not lance > *Remove with tissues*
- Heavy make-up? > Do not apply acid > *apply rosewater*
- Shortened coat? > *Offer free chador*
- Tiny scarf? > Avoid saying: 'Either you cover your head
  or we'll beat your head.' > *Lower the scarf to hide the hair or
  gently trim the hair*

'I've given this paper to all my colleagues,' the salesman tells me, 'so they can show it to the women from
the Revolutionary Guard if they stop one of our customers.'

Before leaving I ask him why he told me to sit down
earlier.

'There's something non-Muslim about the way you
stand,' he tells me.

I don't even try to understand.

'Keep your spirits up!' Davar tells him before turning to
me and saying, 'Tell me, what sort of shape do you think
Fedora's "oriental beret" would be in *La Peau de chagrin*?'

'I haven't a clue. Not like a scarf, that's for sure!'

'The countess was lying full length on a divan,' he
quotes from memory, 'with her feet on a cushion; an oriental beret added an indefinable edge of strangeness to her
seductive charms.'

While I'm trying to think what this beret would look like my mobile rings. It's my aunt.

'Hamid's just come back. He was freed this morning,' she tells me in tears.

An hour later Davar drops me at her house. I'm greeted by Masserat and Samira, whom I kiss, then by Hamid himself who shakes my hand with a smile. My daughter who spends every day with my aunt (I hardly seem to have time to look after her at the moment) jumps into my arms. I go into the living room where Mr Sabeti is lying on the floor with Dr Bashiri walking up and down his back while my uncle watches in fury.

My aunt laughs as she explains, 'Our dear Mr Sabeti broke his back in his efforts to put the satellite dish on the roof of Building C. We dragged him here, but luckily the doctor came and has managed to get him back on his feet.'

For now, though, Mr Sabeti is still on his stomach on the floor.

'*Vay, vay!* Doctor *djan*, have mercy, don't hurt me too much, think about your upgrade.'

'Just a few more moves and I'm done,' replies the doctor, crushing the small of the engineer's back with his foot.

Dr Bashiri, who like me is originally from Mazandaran, has very white skin. My mother always attributed the whiteness of Mazandaranis' skin to the fact that the Arabs, driven back by the harsh conditions in the Alborz mountains, never succeeded in conquering that northern province of Iran or founding a lineage there. Dr Bashiri, who is following the instructions in the Swedish medical magazine, is now in the third phase of the weight loss regime. Which means he has already reduced his intake of food three times. But the privations he's imposing on himself haven't stopped him smiling and baring his dazzling teeth.

Nargess calls me.

'I'm downstairs,' she says. 'I'm taking you to the Asian furniture exhibition.'

Two minutes later Nargess is in the living room. Five minutes later, she's sitting on the floor next to Mr Sabeti, taking her shoes off. She wants to make the most of an opportunity to show Dr Bashiri her *hallux valgus*, an excrescence at the base of her big toe, a physiological oddity which affects a good number of Iranians.

'I had both feet operated on last year, but the bunion on my right foot hurts terribly,' Nargess explains, lifting up her foot.

Sitting firmly astride Mr Sabeti's back, the doctor examines Nargess's toe.

'*Vay, vay*, mercy, doctor *djan*, please,' groans the crushed engineer.

'Did they operate using the Austrian technique?' asks the doctor, ignoring Mr Sabeti's complaints.

Nargess then launches into muddled medical explanations and Dr Bashiri gets to his feet, finally delivering his victim. My aunt invites everyone to stay and eat, and Hamid goes down to get some kebabs. He comes back half an hour later with a tray full of skewers of lamb, grilled tomatoes and basil. In our own quiet way, we're celebrating Hamid's release.

Before he leaves, Dr Bashiri (who must have just brushed his teeth because his breath smells of toothpaste and not kebabs and onions) takes me to one side. I imagine he wants to talk about Hamid. I'm wrong.

'You know,' he whispers, 'for the Adidas thing, we wouldn't even need a contact in the sports industry.'

With one hand on his back and leaning on Hamid, Mr Sabeti leaves slowly, groaning, '*Vay, vay*.'

'All we need to do,' the doctor goes on, 'is get Gérard Depardieu in on it.'

'Who?'

'Gérard Depardieu,' Dr Bashiri says again with a beaming smile. 'Your aunt told me you knew him.'

'So?'

'I read in a cinema magazine that he's made investments in Cuba and various countries from the old Soviet Union. So, as you know him, you could get him in on this.'

My daughter runs over to the door.

'Go away, go away!' she says – in French – to Mr Sabeti who is waiting for the lift. She can't bear having him around because she's deprived of her DVDs and her favourite channels during each upgrading process.

I tell her off and Hamid picks her up in his arms.

From the landing we can hear Mr Sabeti's moans, then the doors closing on the lift as it carries his cries of '*vay, vay*' down towards the silent depths. Mind you, the smell of his eau de cologne is still lingering in the hallway.

Samira hands me the telephone. This time it's the cousin who wants to renew her passport too. I'd forgotten about her.

'Have you had it back?' she asks. 'Your passport, is it all done? Have you got it?'

'No. I've got to wait at least a week.'

'So your guy's not as effective as all that.'

'Like I said . . .'

Just then Dr Bashiri slips some papers into my hand.

'Here, this is for Gérard Depardieu. It's a study of the market potential.'

'What's happened to Depardieu?' my cousin asks, catching a snatch of the doctor's sentence.

'Nothing, nothing.'

'You're so secretive! First you won't give away the name of your contact at the passport office and now you won't tell me what's happened to Gérard!'

I don't know why she's suddenly calling him Gérard.

'My contact's name is Dr Askarnia,' I retort sharply, and give her his phone number.

'It's ultra-confidential, of course,' Dr Bashiri goes on quietly. 'Could you give it to Gérard Depardieu in person?' he adds, waving the papers.

My cousin, who heard everything this time, immediately forgets the number I've given her for her passport.

'What's confidential? Gérard? Is he in Tehran?' she asks.

'No, he's in Cuba,' I say without thinking.

'With Carole?'

Nargess is just passing and asks, 'Have you called Dâryoush?'

'Dâryoush's in Tehran?' says my cousin, more and more astonished.

I can't cope any more. I promise my cousin I'll call her this evening so we can talk about it all properly. Then, so that Nargess doesn't hear, Dr Bashiri whispers in my ear, 'If Gérard Depardieu ever comes to Iran tell him I could also help him with his weight problem. He could follow the same diet as me.'

I promise the doctor I'll get Depardieu to Iran so he can invest in trainers and lose some weight by following this Swedish diet. I also promise Nargess I'll call Dâryoush. I can tell my blood pressure is horribly low. I go into my aunt's bedroom and collapse on the bed. Masserat brings me a mint squash and the phone rings, again and again. I wave my hand, refusing to answer it.

'It's *Monsieur*,' she tells me.

'So what news of your passport?' my husband asks.

'I've got to wait a week. I've already told you that.'

'But that was two days ago. So is it five days now?'

'That's what they've promised.'

A few more words and he hangs up. When I get back to the living room I find Hamid sitting on the floor sticking fake silver-coloured nails on to Kiara's fingers. Nargess is in a hurry: if we don't leave for the Asian furniture show straight away, we'll be stuck in traffic for two hours. I persuade my aunt to come with us: she's been shut away at home since Hamid was arrested. An outing? Well, why not?

A little later the three of us set off to loud protestations from my daughter who feels, once again, she's being abandoned.

The show has been set up in a house in one of the northern districts of Tehran, a building flanked by hanging gardens. Each floor, along with its terrace, evokes a different Asian country. The first floor is decorated with Indian furniture, the second Indonesian, the third Chinese and the fourth Japanese. On each level the music playing and the food on offer are from the same country as the furnishings. Smiling hostesses – all of them Iranian but wearing the traditional dress of each of the countries – tell visitors the musicians' names and explain what is in the various dishes.

In this sort of situation my aunt, who only really sees Mohtaram's children, feels as if she has been projected into another world. She often says that, as far as she's concerned, the normal world is the one of little day-to-day concerns, a place where husbands are fit and active but irascible and demanding (and unfaithful as an optional extra), where children are now grown up and turn themselves inside out worrying about holidays for their own children – thankless temperamental teenagers enslaved by the latest fashion and often drugged up to the eyeballs. That's the world that she comes into contact with and which she sees as the epitome of harmony, even happiness, but, given that she has no children, it's one from which she herself is excluded. This everyday life, the norm everyone else complains about, strikes her as luminous and enviable.

She often tells me how she still gives presents to her friends' children for birthdays, then weddings, when they set up in their first home, have children of their own, the birthdays of this second generation, their weddings, the births of the third generation and so on . . . but never, in fifty years of friendship, has she herself, this childless woman, been given any sort of present. There's never any cause for celebration in her life.

We couldn't be less interested in the Asian furniture, but all of Tehran is here. Most women have taken off their scarves although some, like my aunt, have not. They haven't been to the hairdresser for a while and would rather keep their hair hidden.

'Look at her,' my aunt exclaims, pointing at a tall, upright and elegant older woman. 'She was the most beautiful woman when we were all young. People would go to the restaurant at the Hotel Darband just to look at her.'

The woman in question comes over to me, says hello and asks for news of my husband.

'A long time ago,' she adds, 'I came to your house in Pigalle with Klaus Kinski. I love your husband's work, you know.'

The fact that the elegant woman came up to us to praise my husband delights my aunt.

'You could have told me, I'd have gone to the hair-dresser today,' she chides gently.

We go up to the first floor, the one devoted to India. Here all anyone can talk about is holidays in Goa or Ayuvedic spas in Kerala and Tamil Nadu. A girl I've known since high school is explaining the Sanskrit words *dharma, artha, karma* and *moksha* to some novices. When she sees me (well, I am the wife of the man who adapted *Mahabharata* for Peter Brook) she cuts short her description of these 'four objectives in human life' and, with a new note of humility in her voice, announces, 'Here comes the specialist.'

I refuse to talk about *moksha*. I just want to listen to Ravi Shankar's sita in peace and try the *masala dosa* I've spotted.

On the Indonesian floor the hostess, dressed in multi-coloured batik and wearing strings of pearls and coral in her hair, informs us that the music we're listening to is *Royal Singing* by His Majesty Norodom Sihanouk, and the dish she's offering us is called *pepesan*. I don't risk pointing out that Sihanouk was King of Cambodia and not Indonesia but I do ask her about the ingredients of the *pepesan*. Just like the girls selling Italian fakes, she inhales a narrow lungful of air through her remodelled nose before saying, 'They're wrapped in banana leaves and steamed.'

I don't spend too long on the third floor which honours China. Although I have studied Chinese, I don't speak it well so avoid being introduced to the cultural attaché who doesn't speak a word of Persian and has been waiting all evening for an opportunity to speak in his own language. I manage, not without difficulty, to tear my aunt and Nargess away from the fried noodles and the hostess's explanations about the pipa lute and the musician Liu Fang.

On the last floor the hostess – all done up in a kimono with white make-up and her hair pulled back in a bun – offers us some sashimi. My aunt helps herself with her fingers then grabs a plate and fills it with raw fish.

'Find a way of taking some home for your uncle,' she whispers in my ear.

Equipped with a napkin decorated with Japanese mountains and rivers, I hastily grab some sashimi. My heart's thumping. I hope I haven't been spotted by Klaus Kinski's friend who's coming over.

'This is Nobuko Matsumiya singing. I discovered her through Radio France in Paris. You must know her, don't you?'

I'm holding the hidden sashimi in my hand. I've got to find a way of slipping it into my bag.

'Yes, yes, of course I know her,' I say, moving away.

Another lie.

I rejoin the crowd around Nargess. Some people are asking her for news of her mother, others inviting her to Tuscany, still others wanting to know the name of the best surgeon for removing bunions.

One woman goes up to her and hands her a sample of fabric.

'Where would you say I could find some of this?' she asks her.

Nargess, who always knows everything, kindly informs the woman before turning to me and saying, 'Go and call Dâryoush.'

'*Badan, badan.*'

For once my little voice agrees with Nargess. I shouldn't spend my day in *passajs* and shows without keeping the pressure on Dâryoush. I promise myself I'll stop off at the photo studio on the way home to ask the two photographers to call him. After all, it's thanks to them that I know him.

We go back downstairs but before we leave I go and say hello to the husband of our 'interior designer' hostess.

'All this is to stop my wife getting bored,' he explains, gesturing at the edifice with its hanging gardens, furniture and hostesses in ethnic costumes.

His wife, who hasn't studied architecture for one minute, became an interior designer overnight. Like a good many wives whose husbands earn prodigious amounts of money, she used to do absolutely nothing and was happy that way until a few of her friends started redecorating their own homes, taking their inspiration from pictures in *House and Garden*, *Interiors* and other glossy magazines.

She copied them. Inspired by a special issue on 'internal fountains', she installed one in every room in the house and pronounced herself a designer. Soon less gifted or less reckless friends were consulting her about positioning beds or fabric choices; all of which, naturally, encouraged her to open her own showroom. Now she has clients who own hundreds of newly built apartments that darken the Tehran skyline a little more each day. Her order book is full, and she is quite capable of keeping a customer waiting three years for a swing seat from Mongolia.

She is the one greeting guests by the front door and saying goodbye to them as they leave. She kisses all three of us and we congratulate her on her successful show and particularly on the quality of her sashimi (some of which is hidden in the bottom of my handbag).

Nargess drops me at home and also takes my aunt home.

It feels so nice getting back to my apartment without having to endure Mohtaram's bowing and scraping. Half an hour of solitude and silence, what a blessing.

A little later my aunt sends me Mohtaram and my daughter, who arrives asleep as she does almost every evening. When I put her into my bed I can smell Hamid's cologne.

I turn over, pinching my nose and – quite quickly, I think – fall asleep.

Thursday

Kiara wakes me wailing, 'Mummy, Mummy, the Piwi channel's not working!'

Even before breakfast my day begins with an emergency call to Mr Sabeti for him to upgrade the children's channels. He isn't at home so I leave a message. Then I ring my aunt who will come and pick Kiara up to take her to Tehran's Wonder Land, a real fairyland where a girl of three or four can spend the average office worker's monthly salary in a single day.

Freed from concerns about occupying my daughter, I decide to go to the antique dealers' quarter in Manoutcheri Avenue with Davar. I get into his car, an Iranian Peugeot in which he only ever has French easy-listening music playing.

It is Thursday and that means, by law, we are allowed to go into the centre of Tehran in our own vehicle. The shops on Manoutcheri Avenue are mostly Jewish-owned. I pick one at random and look in the window where, much like any other, trays, samovars, tea glasses, necklaces, rings, coats, medals, manuscripts and old photographs are displayed. Davar leans forwards, picks up a pile of dusty papers and gingerly takes out a yellowed lithograph which probably dates back to the European nineteenth century.

'Look closely,' he tells me. 'You see that woman there. Don't you think she looks like Fedora with that oriental head-dress?'

I look at the woman with her wide bandeau tied behind her head. She's leaning nonchalantly on tasselled cushions, wearing wide silk trousers and flat-heeled clogs, and holding her chin in her right hand. Her open neckline reveals the curve of her breasts and a belt emphasises her narrow waist. A Western image of an oriental woman: idle, sensual, available, as someone might imagine her before actually knowing her.

I ask the salesman whether he happens to have any Iranian nineteeth-century *qadjars* cards decorated with scantily clad women.

In Iran salesmen are slow to help their customers. If they don't sell anything all day (in fact, particularly if they don't sell anything), they still end up better off at the end of the day simply because of the galloping rise in prices. The value of their stock grows all on its own as the hours tick by. They have therefore lost any appetite for selling. Chronic and irremediable depression seems to have descended on them, condemning them, until they are cured, to a vegetative state: getting up in the morning, opening their shops, brewing tea and waiting quietly for the evening to make its slow appearance, without granting their customers any attention at all.

The man whose shop we have ended up in pours himself a glass of tea and offers us some instead of answering my question. I ask it again.

'Everything's here,' he manages, being as unspecific as possible.

Davar, who is still holding the nineteenth-century lithograph, carries on with his observation: 'Actually, when I was quoting Balzac yesterday I forgot a very important sentence about that oriental head-dress.'

He puts the lithograph down on the shopkeeper's untidy desk, shakes the dust from his hand (as if needing to cleanse himself before quoting Balzac), and corrects himself in French, '"*un béret oriental, coiffure que les peintres attribuent aux premiers Hébreux*"[1] . . . that was the little detail I missed out.'

'Where did Balzac get that from?'

Davar has no idea. Which painters? Which Hebrews? A mystery.

The shopkeeper doesn't seem in the least impressed by our French. His melancholic – or rather apathetic – state clearly calls for other remedies. Time weighs heavy on his hands, as it does every day. Above his head a large calligraphy in Persian has pride of place; it reads, 'This too will pass . . .'

It's gone one o'clock and I'm hungry. Davar takes me to a *ghahveh khaneh*, literally a 'coffee house', the sort of mass appeal establishment where, he claims, casting directors pick up their extras.

We go in and, despite the thick fog of hookah smoke, I soon realise I'm the only woman. We choose a table and while we wait to be served I look at the men around me. I spot a *naghal* (a storyteller), an old man with long white hair, an angular face and narrow bony fingers clamped on

---

1 'An oriental beret, a head-dress that painters attribute to the first Hebrews . . .'

a copy of *Shahnameh*, the *Book of Kings*, an ancient Persian
mythical epic. I also see a smiley man of about thirty with
a thick moustache and wearing a short-sleeved shirt
(although short sleeves are not forbidden for men, they are
not advisable) with a neckline revealing the black hairs on
his chest. Further away I notice a group of youngsters
grouped round a hookah, their hands covered in engine
oil. And, to my surprise, I spot my *ajans* driver, the one
with the top of his index finger missing.

As he catches sight of me he jumps to his feet and, stay-
ing where he is, bows slightly as a sign of submission. I
return the greeting.

'Do you know these people?' Davar asks, perplexed.

The driver is now coming over so I do the introductions: 'My friend, Mr Malek, a great writer, and . . .'

'Gheysar, at your service,' the driver adds.

I invite him to sit at our table and he doesn't decline.

'Do you know,' says Davar as he shakes his hand, 'that
Gheysar is the equivalent of Kaiser in German, César in
French and Khosrow in Persian? And they all mean
"emperor".'

The old storyteller, having heard the word 'emperor',
comes over to us and starts reciting from memory the *Book
of Kings* that every Iranian should know.

'The first king was Keyoumars, he taught men to clothe
themselves and feed themselves. Houshang showed them
how to draw metals from stone, mastered fire and invented
the blacksmith's art. Tahmouras instructed men in the arts
of spinning and weaving carpets.'

'You are our *ostad*, our master,' Gheysar whispers in
Davar's ear before sitting down.

The storyteller with the white beard looks me right in
the eye. He sets no store by Islamic restrictions, a bravura

that derives from Iran's glorious past, from the *Book of Kings* that he carries within him like treasure. He most likely knows it by heart from the first to the last line. Clearly admired by everyone present (the room has fallen silent), he intones Ferdowsi's verses.

'Tahmouras domesticated animals. He terraced the land of the *divs* and rode Ahriman as his steed. Djamshid had weapons made, cloth woven and homes and ships built.'

The storyteller is now walking between the tables as he speaks: 'He discovered precious stones, perfumes and remedies. He arranged society into four classes and ensured they lived in peace. But, after a long and glorious reign, he grew proud and arrogant, and divine grace was withdrawn from him. The empire descended into anarchy and Iranian warriors called for an Arab king, Zahhak, who seized the throne, put Djamshid to flight and eventually saw him perish by slicing him in two.'

'*May his soul rest in peace*,' Gheysar adds quietly amid murmurs from neighbouring tables.

The storyteller moves away from us and continues, 'Zahhak was a creature of Eblis, the devil . . .'

We can hardly hear him now.

'I don't want to disturb you, madam,' the driver Gheysar says, 'but if your passport problem hasn't been sorted out yet, I've got a friend here who I'm sure could help you. He knows everyone in the police.'

He points to the thirty-year-old with the moustache and short-sleeved shirt. Seeing us looking at him, the man in question starts to stand up.

'One day,' Gheysar goes on, 'he was taken on as an extra in a detective film and while he was wearing a police sergeant's uniform he left the set to buy some cigarettes.

Out on the street he forgot to salute some real policemen on motorbikes and was promptly arrested.'

A toothless waiter with a red and black cloth over his shoulder and – probably – an opium habit comes over and gives us each some bread dotted with poppy seeds, a plate of onions and basil, a wooden pestle and two bowls, one full of *abgousht* (slow cooked meat) and the other empty.

I feel quite incapable of mixing the ingredients of my *abgousht* as it should be done so Gheysar performs the operation on my behalf: he pours all the liquid into the empty bowl and removes the lamb-tail fat from the other bowl.

'I don't think madam would want that,' he tells Davar.

He uses the pestle and crushes the meat, kidney beans and chick peas in the ceramic bowl. He cuts the bread into small pieces and adds them to the soup. Then he takes the onion and flattens it with one smack of his fist.

'*Befarmayin, noush-e djan*. Help yourself, may your soul take sweet pleasure in it.'

I move the onion aside and when Gheysar notices this he smiles and says, 'I scored a point with the lamb fat but I was caught out by the onion, I got that wrong. And even after I crushed it to make it less pungent.'

When we start eating Gheysar goes back to what he was saying (just as I expected).

'So, how's your passport?'

He reminds me of my husband and his insistent questions on the telephone. This passport's become a sort of linchpin: my whole life revolves around it.

'Still nothing.'

The storyteller is back near us now, two metres from our table. Out of respect for the epic poem, we stop talking.

'The world was subjugated by tyranny, evil reigned. But

revenge was to come in the shape of Fereydoun, the son of one of Zahhak's victims, raised in secret in the mountains.'

The old man points towards Alborz, the mountain range around Tehran. Everyone looks over to where he is pointing.

'One day a blacksmith called Kaveh whose sixteen sons had all been slain by the king joined forces with Fereydoun, roused the people, flew his blacksmith's apron as a standard, fought Zahhak's army and imprisoned him in a crevasse in Mount Damavand.'

'Where is Kaveh the blacksmith? Where is he?' cries one of the young men with engine oil on their hands, before slamming the door of the *ghahveh khaneh* and leaving.

For a moment the storyteller stops talking. Yes, where is he, where is this liberator? We must all be asking ourselves the same thing.

Gheysar waves the actor in the short sleeves over to join us.

'At your service,' the latter says as he sits down at our table.

The waiter clears the bowls of *abgousht* and immediately replaces them with tea served in delicate narrow glasses.

'*Agha* Mahmoud has very good contacts in the police,' Gheysar says, indicating the aspiring thespian.

'And I'm at your service. Tell me what you need.'

I explain briefly that I have submitted a passport renewal form to the passport office in Yaft Abad and am waiting, impatiently, for a reply.

'Yaft Abad?' he asks.

'Yes, Yaft Abad.'

'But Yaft Abad's full of our "children".'

By 'children' (*bar-o batcheh ha*), Mahmoud means his friends, his 'mates'. I'm delighted to think I've found a new source of help in the form of this casual actor, should the (small-scale) lookalike for the singer Dâryoush fail.

Davar is in a hurry because he has a meeting with his editor. As we get up *agha* Mahmoud hands me his card. 'I'm here to be of service to you,' he reiterates. 'Everything's on the card: my mobile, my landline, my email address. Don't hesitate.'

Davar wants to pay but Gheysar, the driver, immediately puts up resistance. The usual *tarof* begins and could go on for ever but I step in and announce in a very firm voice that I must be obeyed.

The storyteller hears me from the other side of the room, and he points to me as he recites another passage from the *Book of Kings*, 'Gordafarid was a woman who compared with a brave horseman. She stood before the entire army like a war-faring man and spoke in a voice like thunder, asking "where are the brave, where are the warriors? Who is prepared to step forward like a croco- dile armed with courage and try himself in combat with me?"'

I wait for the storyteller to finish and bow before him with my arms crossed over my chest. Then I pay the bill and neither Davar nor Gheysar dares thwart me.

Gheysar comes out to Davar's car with us and stands on the pavement until we have left.

'There's a passage in *La Peau de chagrin*, straight after the description of Fedora, in which Balzac says "Her face was imbued with a fleeting charm which seemed to prove that with every passing moment we become new, unique beings bearing no similarities to the *us* of the future or the *us* of the past."'

I compare the *us* of yesterday – the *pepesan*, the old man in his eighties boasting about finding a Japanese singer through Radio France – and the *us* of today – lurching between *abgousht* and the *Book of Kings* in a cheap restaurant.

Still listening to Davar, I study *agha* Mahmoud's card. The photograph of him, featured right in the middle of the card, depicts him with a blue bird on his right shoulder and a yellow one on his left. Over his head the words MAHMOUD'S BIRD SHOP are written in red. To his right, in blue letters, it says CDS OF CANARIES, CDS OF PARROT TRAINING; and to his left, in yellow, WE CURE ALL AVIAN DISEASES.

His mobile number is printed across the bottom of his shirt along with the telephone number and address of his shop: 'Abouzar Square (formerly Fallah Square), beyond the Abouzar mosque, 71 Kolahdouz Avenue (formerly Djafari Avenue).'

I put the card into my handbag, musing on the fact that *agha* Mahmoud, who is only thirty, made a point (as do all Iranians) of giving the old names of the streets which date back to a time when he wasn't even born.

My cousin calls me on my mobile.

'Look,' she says, 'I've been trying to get hold of your doctor all day without any success. The ringtone sounds like he's switched his mobile off for good.'

I'm annoyed with myself for not even trying to call him once, as I should have done. What am I going to tell Nargess?

My cousin checks the doctor's number with me before hanging up with a little note of suspicion in her voice. Perhaps she suspects I've given her a false number.

I don't waste any more time and call Dâryoush, alias Dr Askarnia. The ringtone does sound as if I'm calling a phone that's switched off. I keep trying in spite of myself.

I keep trying if only so that I can tell Nargess he hasn't answered any of my calls.

Should I be worried? I can't tell.

Three minutes later we pass the Ecbatana photo studio. Hassan and Morad are leaning in the doorway. I need only say the word and Davar would stop so I could ask them for news of Dâryoush but, I'm not sure why, I don't. I wave at them and then Davar drops me outside my apartment block.

I call my husband and he tells me he misses me and Kiara. He's worried about my passport and suggests I should still reserve tickets for next Tuesday's flight, just in case.

He's done the maths. Given that I submitted my application on Monday and Colonel Azardel promised me a spanking new passport in a week, I would therefore be able to catch Tuesday's flight if the colonel keeps his promise.

'I'll be expecting you both on Tuesday. And please don't let this business with the passport drag on and on, I really don't understand it at all. Oh, one last thing: don't forget to buy some caviare if you can.'

I immediately call my suppliers: two brothers who sell smuggled goods door to door. An hour later they are on the doorstep in black suits and black hats. They are small, stooped, slightly balding. The first looks like Professor Calculus from *Tintin*, the other has no beard. They are very polite, almost obsequious, and speak quietly as if someone might be listening. Their every move is perfectly coordinated: the first opens his attaché case, the second unscrews the lid on a pot, the first produces a small spoon, the second fills it. I have to taste the contents, and the two men wait for my verdict before moving on to another pot.

The procedure is repeated until I accept the contents of a pot. One asks me how much I would like, the other calculates the price. The first secures the pots together with red adhesive tape, the second covers them in foil. The first closes his attaché case, the second counts the banknotes. When it is over (the transaction has lasted all of ten or fifteen minutes) the two men bid me goodbye and disappear simultaneously.

I've just paid four hundred thousand *tomans* for a kilo of good caviare when the official price in shops in Tehran is a million *tomans* and it's three times that abroad. I try to forestall, to eliminate in advance the anxiety I know I'll feel when I leave with this precious, fraudulently acquired merchandise hidden in my socks and trainers. If I manage to escape the checks at Tehran airport I'll still have to confront the French police and answer the awkward question, 'You've come from Iran, do you have any caviare?'

The videophone rings.

'I've let Mr Sabeti up,' the caretaker warns me.

Mr Upgrade comes in a moment later. I know I should make him some coffee and, as usual in this sort of situation, Mohtaram isn't here.

'When you call me,' he says (and, as ever, he is wearing too much aftershave and is impeccably clean shaven), 'even when you leave a message, I can smell your coffee. You've got me completely addicted to that coffee, I swear it. I can go all over the city and still not find a shop that sells anything like it.'

As I make him his coffee I think to myself that if he succeeds in upgrading Piwi I'll give him another tin of my incomparable coffee. This time it's not my own little voice but Nargess's I can hear chastising me for wasting my money and dangerously spoiling the working classes.

Mr Sabeti, who seems to have recovered from his aches and pains, goes into the library and starts his perennial procedure.

'You should be careful,' he tells me. 'Everyone in the building has taken down their dishes. You and the lady on the nineteenth floor are the only two who've still got them up.'

I picture my neighbour on the nineteenth floor as Gordafarid the valiant, the heroine from the *Book of Kings*. Mr Sabeti quickly adjusts the channels, grumbling about the poor reception created by the authorities with their constant scrambling. Piwi is upgraded; it's done. When I feel the time for payment drawing near, I take my lead from Nargess's recommendations: Don't ask him how much you owe him. You paid him and gave him a tip the day before yesterday to set up channels that we can't watch anyway.

I offer Mr Sabeti a cup of coffee. He savours it and says, '*Bah, bah*, this coffee really is good, I hope I shall drink it at your daughter's wedding.'

From another room I call Nargess to announce proudly that, despite my perseverance and determination, I've failed to get hold of Dâryoush but have managed not to pay Mr Sabeti.

'Call the photographers!' she orders me, not even commenting on my exploits.

'I don't have their number.'

'Go down and see them quickly. It's Friday tomorrow and you won't be able to get hold of anyone.'

'The colonel told me to wait a week. There's still time.'

'In this country "I'll call you in a week" means "you'll have to start hassling me this afternoon". Don't you know that yet?'

' OK, OK. I'll go down and see them.'

'And don't forget to talk about the chairs! It's unacceptable to ask eighty thousand *tomans* for braid that comes unstuck if you so much as breathe on it.'

Mr Sabeti is about to leave but I ask him to wait for me. He offers to drop me somewhere but, perhaps unwisely, I let him know I'm only going next door to the photo studio.

'The Ecbatana studio?'

'Yes.'

'You shouldn't go there alone. Those people don't deserve to be trusted.'

'What makes you say that?'

'Getting into your home on the pretext of delivering chairs, I wouldn't know what to call that sort of thing.'

I try in vain to reassure him. He insists on accompanying me and so it is with him by my side that I step into the Ecbatana studio a few minutes later.

'*Befarmayin*, do sit down,' Hassan invites me.

I sit down while Mr Sabeti stays standing behind me. I tell the photographers that I can't get hold of Dr Askarnia, that his phone seems to be switched off, out of use, and that I've come here in the hope of finding a solution.

'Getting hold of the doctor, it's not easy!' cries Hassan.

'Don't worry,' Morad intervenes, running his hand through his hair yet again. 'I know where he lives. I'll go there myself this evening and I'll let you know what's going on straight away.'

Mr Sabeti, who doesn't know anything about this whole business, leans towards me.

'Would you like me to go too?' he offers.

'No, no,' I say, already regretting giving him the tin of coffee.

A man comes into the studio and Morad bows respectfully as he says, 'I'm afraid we're closed.'

The customer glances over at me sitting on my chair and Mr Sabeti standing behind me. He shrugs his shoulders and leaves without a word. I reckon the photographers have just lost between five and ten thousand *tomans* and decide I won't ever give them a hard time or criticise them for the failings of their braiding.

I'm just getting up when Mr Sabeti suddenly asks Morad, '*Aziz*, dear friend, what's your mobile number?'

I can see Mr Sabeti lives in the same country as Nargess. They speak the same language where 'I'll let you know what's going on straight away' means 'you'll have to keep pestering me and call me every half-hour'.

We go out, equipped with Morad's number. Mr Sabeti leaves, watched resentfully by the two photographers. On the doorstep Morad asks me whether the upgrade was successful. When I say it was, he looks amazed.

I go back up to the apartment to try and work on my conference about the Buddhist nature of Iranian Sufism. I sit at my father's desk – the selfsame one at which he translated into Persian al Nadim's *Fihrist*, the famous Arab catalogue of the tenth century – and spread out the books which will help me write my own speech: a collection of Attar's poems, the *Djame-o-tawarikh*, and Buddhist texts such as the *Dighanikaya* and the *Majjhimanikaya*.

I work intensively for more than an hour. The *Majjhimanikaya* says 'O monks, there are two extremes that the faithful must avoid: attachment to pleasures and attachment to mortifications.' In the *Mantegh-o teyr* (*The Conference of Birds*) Attar uses almost the same words: 'If the door opens before me, there is no distinction between blasphemy and faith. For behind the door neither the one nor the other exists.'

The door opens and my daughter appears, transformed into a tiger by face-painting. Her cheeks are striped with huge mauve whiskers. She's exhausted and exhilarated. All I can think is how difficult it's going to be cleaning her up before bed.

Friday

This Friday I've decided to visit my father's grave at Behesht Zahra, Tehran's vast cemetery. Davar recommends going by underground.

'Take a taxi to Mir Damad,' he says, 'and you can go straight from there. It'll take an hour at the outside.'

One of my aunt's principal occupations is helping out Hamid and Mohtaram's entire family, so she has taken on Mohtaram's husband Hashem to act as my chauffeur. Hashem is a diminutive seventy-year-old who, despite his age and Iranian genetic inheritance, still has the same head of hair as in his youth. All the elements of his face seem to obey some centripetal movement: every line leads towards the tip of his nose. At a quick glance (will he forgive me this?), it's like seeing a chihuahua's head on a man's body.

Given that driving in Tehran's town centre is forbidden for individuals, all Hashem can do is take Kiara from my apartment to my aunt's and vice versa, a trip which in normal conditions takes about five minutes by car. The only day he can be of any use to me is Friday. Now Friday isn't a working day and Hashem likes to spend it with his wife, a long way from where I live. This week I warned him I was planning to go to Behesht Zahra, so he is happy to forego their time together, this once.

Once we have dropped Kiara and Mohtaram outside my aunt's apartment block Hashem starts showing off his entire English vocabulary to me (he boasts about the fact that, for his first boss, he used to drive the only Bentley in Tehran and that he worked as *maître d'* in the classiest restaurant in the Pahlavis' capital, where he used to deploy these English words on all the Americans who lived there).

'Hashem *agha*,' I interrupt him, panicking at the thought of wasting too much time, 'we're not on the right motorway. Take the next exit.'

'Spoon, knife, fork.'

'Hashem *agha*, slow down, just don't miss this exit!'

'Napkins, chicken, cucumber.'

The whole vocabulary gets an airing, or almost . . . And, of course, we miss the exit.

It's already two hours since we set off and we've barely left Tehran. Hashem likes talking politics. He listens attentively to the news and gives his opinion on every subject. Like all his fellow Iranians, he is in favour of Iran enriching its uranium, although he doesn't actually understand the technical significance of this term or its possible consequences. Mind you, to be honest, I don't know what 'enriching uranium' means either.

On the subject of the bomb, his theory is simple and can be summarised thus: if the bomb isn't a good thing then why do the others, the world's superpowers, have it?

He asks that question once a day.

Today, having just missed another exit, he adds, 'How can we accept that Iran hasn't got the bomb when those dusky Indians and Pakistanis have? Mmm? How can we accept that?'

Thanks to a huge traffic jam, we're now stuck. I open the window and ask the driver of another Peykan the way to the Behesht Zahra cemetery.

'Take the next exit and go back the other way. You've come too far.'

'I used to have an Indian working for me,' Hashem goes on, unperturbed. 'His skin was so dark we didn't even let him wait on tables.'

He puts his indicator on and finally takes an exit.

'Way out,' he announces proudly in English.

We pass Imam Khomeyni's mausoleum with its four minarets around a huge dome covered in gold. The building work is still not finished and this is clear from the four turquoise-coloured domes masking the buildings which will soon be receiving delegates for seminars.

We drive into Behesht Zahra at last. I buy some rose-water and flower petals, and we go over to the building which houses my father's tomb. We're finally here after three hours' journey, when the underground station is twenty metres from the family grave.

You should have listened to Davar, whispers my little voice.

This funeral monument was confiscated, along with the rest of our assets, by the Islamic ruling power. I carried on coming here despite the locked gates, despite the fact that the tomb became a store for municipal building materials. One morning, when bulldozers were flattening neighbouring buildings, I stood here staring at the bags of cement hiding my father's gravestone, and emptied myself of my own country.

After that, whenever anyone called me from Iran I didn't

dare ask whether the bulldozers had finished their work. But one day I got a phone call from my niece (who is old enough to be my mother because my father married twice: he had his first son when he was seventeen and his last child, me, when he was seventy-four). She was ringing to tell me she'd managed not only to reclaim the tomb but to have it renovated. The bulldozers clearing the entrance to Imam Khomeyni's mausoleum had stopped a few metres short of our monument.

'I've got a key for you. You can go there whenever you want,' she told me.

I have the key in my hand today. Now at last, after thirty years, I can kiss my father's tomb once more.

Hashem calls over a cemetery employee to sweep the inside, then recites the prayer for the dead and leaves me alone. I pour some rosewater on the windows and walls and the marble of the gravestone, then cover the floor with petals. I kneel on the stone and whisper to my father that I now have a daughter and am reconciled with Iran.

A little further on is the Square of Martyrs where victims of the Iran–Iraq war are laid to rest. The families of the fallen often have picnics on the tombs of their lost loved ones. I risk wandering through a labyrinth of windows erected over each tomb, sealing in the marytrs' personal effects. A young woman born after the war has come to introduce her husband to her brother who died at the front. A solitary widow removes the cover protecting the glass box, opens the lock and gently picks up the photograph of a young man of twenty. She kisses it and whispers a few words to him. She could be his mother now. Her face is angular and her nose hooked – she's not one of the women stampeding to have their noses fixed. She has full lips and magnificently prominent cheekbones.

She takes the end of her chador to dry her tears from the frame before putting it back in its place. She picks up the dead man's watch, wipes the dust from its face, smells the leather of the strap and winds it up. Then she adds two artificial roses to the bouquet of plastic flowers.

My mobile rings. I don't want to answer but I can see that it's Morad. I move a little way away. The widow gives me a reassuring wave to show that I'm not disturbing her.

'Hello, hello, I can't hear you very well!' bellows the photographer.

'*Agha* Morad, try and get me later. I'm at Behesht Zahra, I can't talk.'

'Where?'

'Behesht Zahra. At the cemetery.'

'Have you got a pen and paper?'

Quickly I open my bag and its entire contents spill on to the *shahid*'s grave. I apologise to the widow, who patiently hands me my lipstick, notebook, bar of chocolate and comb.

'*Agha* Morad, I can't find my pen. Try calling me later.'

'Do you need a pen?' the widow asks, getting to her feet. I nod.

'Write this down,' Morad goes on. 'Six photos, latest phone or electricity bill, ID card plus a photocopy of it.'

'But I've already supplied those documents to the office in Yaft Abad!' I exclaim, backing away.

'Don't move! I can't hear you any more,' cries Morad. I go back towards the tomb.

'Yes, it's better there,' he says.

'I said I've already provided those documents.'

'No, no. This is for your *kart-e melli*.'

'*Agha* Morad, I can't stress enough how urgently I need to get hold of Dr Askarnia.'

'I've just spoken to him, he's the one who's offering to help you get the *kart-e melli*.'

'But I don't want a *kart-e melli*! I want my passport!'

'Well, write down this number.'

'Say that again,' I ask him, trying to remember the numbers by heart.

Just then the widow slips her hand inside the window on the grave. Quite naturally she takes out a biro which once belonged to the young martyr, and hands it to me. I move my hand closer to hers, hesitating to take the pen. I almost feel I'm committing some sort of sacrilege.

'Write, write! Pens are made for writing with!' insists the widow.

I do as I'm told and start writing down the number. But the biro resists, it's run dry. I try again, pressing hard and scribbling. The pen finally gives in and lets me write the numbers down in a shaky hand.

I can hear Morad fairly well, although he is having trouble hearing me.

'If you want to contact Dr Askarnia,' he says, 'hello? this is the number you need to ring. Hello? hello?'

I have the pen in my hand. It's as if I can feel the young man's heart beating between my fingers, the martyr who fell on 2 khordad 1361,[2] fighting to reconquer Khorramshahr, an oil town in the south.

I hang up and thank the widow. When I hand back the pen she asks whether I'd like to share her lunch with her but I decline her invitation. She puts the biro back in the box and picks up her husband's prayer beads, Koran and ritual clay tablet to recite the funeral prayer.

I leave her in privacy and get back to Hashem's car. He

2 May 1982.

bombards me relentlessly all through the return journey:
'Food, bill, tip . . .'

My husband calls, worrying about our daughter this
time.

'If you've got to stay there any longer,' he says, 'you
should take Kiara to the country. How can you keep a
child shut up in a little apartment all day, surrounded by
old people and all that pollution?'

He's right. I decide to go and pick Kiara up and take her
for a walk in a park. I call Nargess to ask her to join us.

'We should go to Sad Abad Park,' she suggests. 'It's not
as crowded as the public parks.'

The Sad Abad complex was built by Reza Shah, the
founder of the Pahlavi dynasty, and it includes his own
palace as well as those of his son, Mohammad Reza Shah,
and various princes. The Revolution turned these palaces
into museums and there is an entry fee which discourages
the Friday crowds from filling the park with samovars,
wood-burners, pots of rice and badminton rackets.

Even though Nargess lives near Sad Abad, she offers to
come and pick me up. I refuse the offer.

'But the roads are fine on Fridays!' she retorts. 'And
I'm in the car already.'

So I have to do as I'm told. Twenty minutes later Mr
Eskandari tells me, via the videophone, that Nargess is
there. I can't wait to tell her I've finally secured the right
phone number for Dâryoush. When I get downstairs and
into her car she doesn't give me time to announce my
minor victory.

'Before you do anything else, call Dâryoush,' she orders.

Which I do, obediently. In vain: there's no reply.

'It's odd,' I say. 'Morad gave me this new number and
promised he'd answer.'

'Did you get hold of Morad?'

'Just this morning, at Behesht Zahra.'

'And didn't you call straight away?' she asks, apparently dismayed.

'I didn't think his number would change in a couple of hours!'

'Put it on automatic redial and keep your mobile on you,' she instructs me.

I obey her, yet again.

Hamid and Kiara are standing outside my aunt's apartment block waving at us wildly. Kiara gets on to the front seat with me and, as the people of Tehran say, we head 'up' north. Having taken so many foreign friends to visit Sad Abad I know the place almost by heart: each building, the date it was built and the position of all the precious objects. My daughter's particularly excited at the thought of walking through palaces which belong to the king, the queen and princesses. She looks everywhere for them, in every corner. We have to buy a ticket and go into the Shah's palace to show her pictures of the sovereigns.

'Where's the queen?' she keeps asking.

'She doesn't live here any more,' I tell her.

'And the king?'

'He's dead.'

'Is he with your mummy, on the moon?' she asks.

'Yes.'

'Why's your mummy dead?'

'Because she was ill.'

'And was the king too?'

'Yes, the king was too.'

We go into the empress's bedroom where a warden, a young woman of about thirty, is putting some flowers in a vase.

'I do this every day,' she explains softly. 'It's my own way of showing her my respect.'

'Isn't the queen here any more?' asks Kiara.

'I hope this flower will make her come back,' the warden replies.

I think back to Balzac's words and the comparison between the *us* of the future and the *us* of the past, between the young martyr's glass box and the empress's dressing table.

On the way home, while I cancel the automatic redial and try Dâryoush's number again, we go over all the latest gossip in Tehran. Dâryoush, despite the new number, is still impossible to get hold of.

'Call Morad,' Nargess suggests.

I do. Morad isn't answering either.

'Let's go to the studio,' she decides, wanting to get this waiting over.

'It's Friday, it's closed. There's no one there.'

'We'll get them to come, anyway, those thieves. Eighty thousand *tomans* for that crap braid . . .'

She finds a parking space quite easily and we walk to the Ecbatana studio.

'Where are the thieves?' Kiara asks.

Her day couldn't have been more exciting. After visiting the king's palace she's now being asked to infiltrate a pirates' lair.

It's dark, the street is deserted and the metal shutters on all the shops are down. We buy some plums and green almonds from a street vendor and sit down by a water-course to wait for the highly improbable − not to say miraculous − appearance of the photographers.

'Where are the thieves?' my daughter asks again.

'I wouldn't mind a word with them,' says Nargess, hardly in the mood for laughing.

Half an hour goes by. Convinced we're wasting our time, I use the fact that it's Kiara's bedtime as an excuse to get up. But my daughter resists the move, determined to meet the thieves.

'Go home if you want to,' Nargess says. 'I'm waiting here. You'll see, they'll show up in the end.'

Go home? Stay here? I'm dithering. My mobile rings and it's Dr Bashiri.

'Nahal *khamoum*, have you had a look at the confidential document for Gérard Depardieu?'

I've just realised that I left the thing at the Asian furniture show. I must have put it down somewhere, probably when I was pocketing the sashimi for my uncle.

Come on then . . . I'm not going to be put off by a little lie.

'Yes,' I tell the doctor. 'I don't know much about that sort of thing but it looks very interesting. Don't worry, I'll give it to him myself.'

When I look up, Morad is standing in front of me: he's just arrived. Nargess was right to wait.

'What's going on? What's happened?' he asks, rather embarrassed.

Nargess gets up and I copy her.

'Is he the thief?' asks Kiara.

'No, no. *Agha* Morad's a photographer.'

'*Agha* Morad . . .' Nargess begins in a serious voice.

'Excuse me,' Morad says to me, 'but who is this lady?'

'*Agha* Morad,' Nargess goes on, ignoring the photographer's question, 'this passport business absolutely has to be cleared up tomorrow.'

I can hear the white-bearded storyteller celebrating the bravery of Gordafarid, Iran's legendary heroine. There's a manifestation of her right here, standing next to me in the street: 'She stood before the entire army like a war-faring man and spoke in a voice like thunder, asking "where are the brave, where are the warriors? Who is prepared to step forward like a crocodile armed with courage and try himself in combat with me?"'

'We've done absolutely nothing wrong,' retorts Morad irritably. 'All we've ever tried to do at every stage is help you. Just help, that's all. Is this how people repay a favour these days?'

'What favour?' Nargess cries.

'Is he the thief?' Kiara insists, tugging my clothes enthusiastically.

'*Agha* Morad,' I say, gesturing towards Nargess, 'Mrs Dadvar is more than a friend, she's a *delsouz*, someone who would have her heart burned out to stand by her friends.'

'I would just like to point out that here, on this street, Hassan and I enjoy a degree of prestige. Is it appropriate for two women and a little girl to come and sit outside our studio on a Friday evening accusing us of goodness knows what?' he asks.

'Don't get things all mixed up,' I say rather awkwardly. 'Listen to me, *agha* Morad . . .'

He runs his hand over his forehead in agitation so I hand him the bag of green almonds.

'We only came down to buy some *tchaghalehs*,' I add. 'Have some, please.'

'Well, only because it's you,' he says, accepting a few almonds.

'Before we go our separate ways, would you be so kind as to get hold of Dr Askarnia? Or would that be too much to ask?'

Morad sits on the parapet beside the watercourse, lights

a cigarette, gives a deep sigh and, lowering his voice, begins his explanation.

'Actually, Colonel Azardel has fallen out with the doctor.'

'What do you mean?'

'Just like I said.'

I'm devastated. I think about ringing my husband to say he shouldn't bank on my being there for Venice or Cannes, not this year nor the next.

'What did they fall out over?' asks Nargess.

'The medical examination of his cousin's body, which was carried out by the doctor, really upset the colonel.'

'How did it upset him?'

'I'm sorry but I don't know any of the details.'

'Are they not talking to each other?'

'No. The colonel's refusing to see the doctor again. Because of the conclusions of the autopsy. That's all I know.'

I wonder anxiously what those conclusions might have been. Were traces of drugs found in the cousin's body? Or signs of illicit copulations?

'And what are we going to do now?' Nargess goes on.

'He'll explain that himself. I'll call him.'

Morad takes his mobile, dials a number and puts me through to Dâryoush at last.

'Nahal *djan*,' he says, 'I haven't heard from you for such a long time. Last year I was your friend, but this year I'm just an acquaintance.'

'No you're not. What are you talking about, doctor?'

'You've forgotten all about us!'

'What do you mean I've forgotten you? I haven't stopped calling you for two whole days! And there was never any reply!'

'I know, I know. I went to Tabriz with the funeral convoy just for you, just so I could go on pleading your case! But, well, there's no point pursuing things with Colonel Azardel. That's just the way it is. Because of the conclusions of the autopsy, would you believe.'

'What can I do then?' I ask, thinking of my old passport with holes punched through it.

If it weren't for these wretched photographers I would have had a chance, like everyone else, of queuing on the street for forty-eight hours and a guarantee of a new passport within a month.

'Listen,' Dâryoush rallies, as if racked with regret, 'bring me six ID photos tomorrow. Have them done by Morad . . .'

'Why six ID photos?'

'For your *kart-e melli*. You really have to have that card.'

'No, I don't want a *kart-e melli*. It's my passport I want! I really have to get out of Iran! I've got to go to France.'

'Why are you turning this down?' Nargess whispers. 'Ask him for your *kart-e melli* as well. What is there to lose?'

'I'll do something else for you,' the doctor adds. 'Listen . . . Meet me at ten o'clock sharp tomorrow morning at the gates of the Central Passport Office. Have you got that? Ten o'clock exactly.'

He hangs up.

'Where's the thief?' Kiara asks again.

'Kiara, this man's not a thief, he's a photographer. In fact we're going to come back here so he can take a picture of us.'

'It would be my pleasure,' says Morad.

I pat him gently on the shoulder and smile at him to dispel any misunderstandings.

'See you tomorrow, *Khanoum koutchoulou*, little lady,' he says to my daughter who is still convinced she's met a thief disguised as a photographer.

We head off in different directions. Nargess doesn't want to come up to the apartment.

'After all that, you didn't let me sort out the problem with the chairs,' she grumbles bitterly.

'*Badan, badan*, later, later.'

Saturday

This morning, like every other morning, my first telephone call is to my aunt. I explain that I've finally managed to get through to Dâryoush, that all is not lost and I'm meeting him at ten o'clock outside the Central Passport Office against my husband's wishes and will leave my daughter at her house.

Ten minutes later she calls me back.

'Come and pick me up. I've spoken to your uncle and he thinks it would be a good idea if I met this Dâryoush too. You never know, he could be useful to us one day.'

How can I tell her that, since the unfortunate outcome of Colonel Azardel's cousin's autopsy, Dâryoush is now disgraced in the eyes of the Central Passport Office? Too complicated. Too many unanswered questions. I don't risk going into it.

'I'll be with you in half an hour.'

I drag my daughter from her pots of paint and brushes, take off her painting overall and try to dress her in something other than pink. In vain. Pink is her favourite colour, her only colour. She has a *vie en rose*, a life in pink.

I find Hashem and Mohtaram in the kitchen. Hashem is planning to come with me in the hope of putting his English to use. I remind him that I'm going 'to town' (an expression that's stayed with me since my childhood when we lived in Shemiran to the north of Tehran), and that he really ought to know by now that private cars are strictly forbidden there.

'We could always find a way of avoiding the police,' he says, probably dreaming of going over the English names of kitchen utensils for me.

I take a sip of my coffee, Mr Sabeti's favourite, and give him my reply.

'No, that's impossible.'

Mind you, I do know that it is possible. Nargess does it all the time, quite happily. She has her circuit. She knows exactly where each policeman is stationed round the perimeter beyond which traffic is banned. By adeptly avoiding them, she manages to drive her own car all over Tehran.

The phone rings and I tell Mohtaram to say I'm not here.

'It's from abroad,' she whispers.

'I haven't got time to talk.'

'Telefon laterr, hello, telefon laterr,' she says in English before hanging up.

Hashem, who can't bear Mohtaram's progress in mastering foreign languages, announces solemnly, 'Mohtaram khanoum, "telefon" is a Persian word. When you say "telefon laterr" to a Frenchman he doesn't understand a thing. If you don't know how to say "telefon" in English you'll have to just say "laterr".'

He pours me some more coffee and solicits my support.

'Madam,' he begs, 'try to make her understand that

speaking a foreign language doesn't just mean dropping in the odd word.'

'Dropping in the odd word' is a reference to the French words Mohtaram has learned since she's been looking after my daughter. Hashem, who is dominated in every field by his wife, can't bear the fact that she is now even overtaking him in his own area of competence – languages.

'The other day,' he goes on, 'Mohtaram said, "I'm going to make some *pâtes*[3] for Kiara *khanoum*." The woman spends less than a month with a French-speaking child and she forgets her own vocabulary. Mohtaram *khanoum*, for *pâtes* we Persians say macaroni.'

'*Boro baba*, leave me alone,' retorts Mohtaram, who gave up stooping to her husband's level long ago.

As far as Mohtaram is concerned there is only one ideal, one aim in life: behaving and thinking like my mother whom she served for many, many years and still sees as a supreme model. Just like my mother, Mohtaram can't abide chitter-chatter, switches off the radio in the car, loathes floral arrangements (my mother would instantly snip the elastic throttling flowers and arrange them freely in a vase), drinks tea in a cup barely half full, avoids embracing anyone, pinches her nose when confronted with strong perfume . . .

Making the most of Mohtaram's apparent indifference, Hashem repeats, 'To us Iranians it's macaroni, not *pâtes*.'

I look at my watch and, even though I'm in a hurry to leave, I pursue the subject.

'Hashem *agha*, "telefon" and "macaroni" are both foreign words.'

He doesn't look convinced. I blunder on, trying to give

3 pasta.

him technical explanations: 'You know the telephone was invented by Graham Bell who was an American scientist.'

'It doesn't matter who invented it! The word's Persian.'

'*Boro baba,*' Mohtaram tells her husband again, then she turns to me and, as she washes up my cup, says, 'Don't bother, madam, it's no use.'

Hashem opens the cupboard, takes out a box of *farfalle* pasta and says, 'Look, read it, it's written in Persian. Look there . . . "Macaroni"!'

'Hashem *agha,*' I say, 'it's beneath you and your international culinary knowledge not to know that macaroni is an Italian word used only for tubular-shaped pasta.'

He takes a few *farfalle,* looks at them closely and, with a degree of insolence, insists, 'Macaroni is a Persian word used for a variety of different shapes, including this butterfly wing shape.'

I'm not sure what to say. On the box of Iranian-produced *farfalle* I can actually see the words 'butterfly macaroni'. Hashem is right. I have to admit it.

And now I'm late. I run and get ready, putting on correct Islamic dress for the sake of the staff of the Central Passport Office. Mohtaram takes care of calling for an *ajans,* a job she would in no circumstances entrust to Hashem whom she deems incapable of 'ordering a taxi properly' – in spite of his recent etymological triumph.

She's waiting for me by the door with my scarf, which she has ironed.

'Don't worry about Kiara,' she says quite loudly, 'I'll give her some *pâtes* at lunchtime.'

The *ajans* driver is neither Gheysar nor the one who doubles the price of every trip. Today's has blue eyes (I wonder whether he's wearing contacts by any chance), a surgically enhanced nose and rebellious hair, Johnny Depp style.

I give him the name of my aunt's building: ASP. He stares at me in the rearview mirror.

'I'm sorry,' he says. 'I don't know where that is.'

Everyone in Tehran knows those buildings, the first residential tower blocks in the capital, built in the Shah's day by French engineers. I tell him how to get there.

Warned by Mohtaram, my aunt is waiting for us at the bottom of the stairs. She gets into the *ajans* and we ask the driver to take us to the Central Passport Office.

'I'm sorry, I don't know where it is,' he says.

'You are driving an *ajans*, aren't you?' my aunt asks irritably.

'Yes, but I'm not a taxi driver.'

'What do you do then?' she enquires.

He eyes me in the rearview mirror again and says, 'I'm a steward on internal flights.'

OK. Another little mystery I don't have time to elucidate. We direct him road by road, motorway by motorway, all the way to our destination. Once there, I ask him to wait for us.

'Could I inconvenience you for a moment?' he asks me.

'Yes, what is it?'

'If you've got some way of getting inside there, could you ask for a passport form for me?'

'Do you want to leave Iran, then?'

'Who doesn't?'

Dâryoush is there, outside the iron gate. I introduce him to my aunt.

'She must have broken a lot of hearts in her day,' he whispers in my ear.

'What does the doctor want?' she asks, having not heard. I don't know what to say: my aunt is one of those rare women who doesn't appreciate men's compliments. In her youth, when she really could break hearts, she was happy to gaze at her husband alone, and tolerated praise only from my father, her brother-in-law. One night in the 1960s in the legendary nightclub of Tehran's Darband Hotel she was asked to dance by the Casanova of the time. With one quick glance she got her husband's permission and, despite her own misgivings, accepted the invitation of this supposedly irresistible seducer.

Committed to the dance floor almost in spite of herself, she immediately orchestrated a security zone between her partner and herself by keeping her hands at breast height, and she danced liked that right to the end of *E viva España*. To this day she likes describing how she suffered through that *paso doble* all those years ago. To avoid meeting her partner's eyes (which were more beautiful than her husband's) she pinned her own eyes on the floor and almost fell over several times. Drops of sweat rolled down her face. She tried to clap out the rhythm with her clammy hands but they kept slipping. All through this quasi-bull-fighting combat, she saw herself as the bull being brought down by the most handsome man in Tehran under the sympathetic – but ultimately complicit – eyes of their fellow nightclubbers. When the song ended her partner kissed her hand and she rubbed it so furiously against her red skirt she might have been trying to rub off a stain. She even blocked her ears when he murmured the words, 'You're so beautiful.'

What could I tell her now? That Dâryoush thought she was beautiful?

'Nothing. Let's go this way,' I say, leading her to the booth where women's clothing is checked.

When I open my handbag to show it to an inspector,

the woman waves at me to close it again and offers me a plate of dates.

'Help yourself. Don't bother with the *tarof*,' she adds. 'They're good for your blood pressure.'

She glances quickly at my aunt's clothes and explains to her, 'Your daughter was so pale last time . . . I had to insist she sat down and had a glass of sweetened tea.'

I realise that it is indeed the same woman inspector as last week. I wonder how she can have recognised me given that, since our brief meeting, she must have checked the fingernails, lips, handbags, scarves and coats of several thousand women.

I congratulate her for her memory. She offers me the dates again and I take a couple and go out of the booth with my aunt. Dâryoush takes us over to the ground-floor concourse where passports can be picked up. He suggests we each queue at a different window.

At that exact moment I know for sure that Dâryoush is no longer helping us, that I can't count on him any more. We choose three separate queues and wait. My aunt, who has a bad back, quickly abandons the exercise. Dâryoush tells the woman in front of him that he's slipping away for a moment but will be back straight away. He's going to get supplies of cakes and drinks, he explains. He comes back a moment later with some 'exotic juice' and a box of cream puffs. We haven't moved a muscle. My aunt throws herself on a pastry.

'*Noush-e djan*,' Dâryoush says, 'may your soul take sweet pleasure in it.'

I want to pay, which is perfectly normal.

'Aren't you ashamed? Do you want to dishonour me or something?' exclaims Dâryoush, pushing away my money.

I put it back in my bag. Dâryoush generously offers the

box of cream puffs round the people near us. Struck down by a contagious *tarof*, they all refuse to touch them. Dâryoush puts a straw into the exotic fruit juice and asks me whether I've tasted it before.

'All of Europe's addicted to products made by this Iranian brand,' he adds.

'No, I've never tried it.'

'Go on, have some, *noush-e djan*. Stop thinking about your work and your conference the whole time . . . Go on, drink it.'

I try his exotic fruit juice which tastes like any other exotic juice the world over. Then I stand on tiptoe to catch sight of the policeman, who's leaving his position with files under his arms.

'That one's just left,' I tell Dâryoush. 'Can't we go up and see Colonel Azardel?'

'I really must deal with your *kart-e melli*,' he says in reply, as if he hadn't heard me mention the colonel. 'If you like, when we've finished here, I can take you to a colleague who can sort it out in half an hour.'

Kart-e mellis are usually obtained after six months of complex and exhausting manoeuvring with the Post Office, the bank and Tehran's main municipal offices. I quite understand that Dâryoush's insistence about my *kart-e melli* is a veiled admission of his powerlessness in the case of my passport.

He runs through the names stored in his mobile.

'Here,' he says, 'write down this number. Tell Mr Zargar I gave you his number and tell him it's about your *kart-e melli*.'

'I'm very grateful but right now I only really need my passport.'

'My goodness, you're stubborn! Like all depressives! Mr Zargar's a valuable colleague, he's a one-off!'

He brings his hand up to his pursed lips and mimes blowing this Mr Zargar a kiss.

'And, actually, if you'd brought your papers with you, I could have given them to him later, at the morgue.'

By deliberately forgetting my documents I've just spared my six photographs, my latest electricity bill, and the original and photocopy of my ID card from being put on to the stomach of a corpse, somewhere between the oesophagus and the duodenum.

My aunt, who's just finished her cream puff, seizes this opportunity to discuss her husband's case with the pathologist.

'Dr Askarnia, my husband's going to need to renew his passport soon too. But he can't get out of the house so I wondered whether you would know anyone who can help us.'

'Why can't he get out of the house?'

My aunt never uses the words 'handicapped', 'invalid' or 'infirm' so she says, 'the surgeon who operated on his slipped disc pulled him about so much that my husband has temporarily lost the use of his legs.'

'So beautiful and living with a paraplegic!' Dâryoush whispers to me.

'I'm so sorry, Dr Askarnia, I didn't quite hear that,' says my aunt, her eyes already full of tears.

'And so sensitive, too!' Dâryoush adds.

When it's his turn, Dâryoush calls me over to the window and gives me his place in the queue. I slip the receipt from the office in Yaft Abad through a slot for the officer sitting in a glass cage. He studies it and tells me I'll have to wait at least a month for my passport.

I turn round, locate Dâryoush and wave him over, but he drags his feet: since the colonel stopped talking to him he no longer has any leverage at the Central Passport Office – and he knows it. Rumours of who is in and out of favour travel fast. Still, he slowly comes over to join me at the counter, offers the officer a cream puff and some exotic fruit juice, and tells him surreptitiously that my case was being handled by Colonel Azardel.

The officer refuses the pastry but gets up to take the fruit juice and says, 'Well, in that case, tell him to give me written instructions.'

Dâryoush presses his face up to the window and mutters confidentially, 'The colonel is in mourning, perhaps you knew that. I can't disturb him for something this minor. *Dearest to my heart*, why don't you have a look on your computer. I'm convinced her passport is ready.'

The officer clatters away on his keyboard for a moment, then looks up at me.

'There's a problem,' he says.

'What?'

'The passport's been blocked by Section 1.'

'Section 1?' Dâryoush asks in amazement, taking a step back.

'Exactly,' replies the officer.

Being refused by Section 1 is the worst form of sanction. It's the equivalent of a formal ban on leaving Iranian soil. This section, which handles only affairs of national security, is something of an obsession for all Iranians, for anyone who may have done anything, however tenuous, to rock the Islamic regime.

What's happened? Why has my passport ended up being denied by Section 1? I scan the room for my aunt and am happy to see her enjoying another cream puff. I take courage: she's a long way away and busy putting on weight that even the Swedish magazine would have trouble getting her to shift. She therefore won't be passing out at news of my prolonged – or even definitive – stay in Iran.

I hastily try and envisage the reasons why my file might have been turned down by Section 1. Sometimes just a picture in a bikini beside a pool, a hug from a friend in the antiques market, a roar of laughter at the Arts Foundation, too big a balloon of bubblegum on the bus, a red umbrella opened on a rainy day, a sweet eaten during the month of Ramadan, a visit from two *na mahrams* (men who are not family members) over a glass of tea – sometimes just things like that can be interpreted as subversive acts, endangering the stability of the regime and the very basis of Islam.

Again hastily, I conclude that I can be accused of all these crimes, or almost, and, paradoxically, I react as if I'm quite beyond reproach: I slam my fist down on the counter in front of the officer and shout (which is something I never normally do).

'I can't possibly have any problems with Section 1!' I say. 'It's impossible!' and I bring my fist down again.

I turn round to consult Dâryoush but, afraid he will be further compromised by being with me (he's on the wrong side of Colonel Azardel, don't let's forget), he hangs back, a few paces away, as if he can't see me.

I drum the counter once more and cry out again as loudly as I can, 'Do I need to say it again: it's just not possible that Section 1 has rejected my passport application! How many times do I have to say that?'

I can hear my own voice which I suddenly don't recognise. It's no longer the voice of the woman who responds so meekly to iniquity, is referred to as 'defenceless', just sighs in the face of misfortune and lets herself be influenced by her characteristic reserve, her upbringing and goodness.

The voice I'm hearing is my mother's, a powerful, determined, intrepid voice. I can suddenly see my mother, single-handedly defending the last parcel of her estates from revolutionary farm-workers. I can see her, as a younger woman, in the village square surrounded by land that she owned, confronting an emissary from the Shah's brother, and slapping him across the face. I can see her crossing a river in full spate on horseback at night. I can see her as a child, dressed in military uniform with her pet tiger by her side, reviewing her father's troops – her father the Kurdish general whose ancestors were posted to Mazandaran in the sixteenth century at the request of the Safavid kings to safeguard Iran's northern borders.

The officer sips his exotic fruit juice as he consults his computer.

'Why are you screaming?' he asks me dolefully. 'There's no point upsetting everyone. People can make mistakes, can't they?'

'Did you make a mistake?'

'You're so impatient! Let me explain.'

He swallows a mouthful of juice. I think to myself that with his black lips and languid elocution he must be an opium addict.

'In fact, your passport is still in Yaft Abad.'

Still suffering the shock of Section 1, Dâryoush is keeping his distance from me.

'Dr Askarnia,' I call over to him, 'come here. The problem is that my passport's stayed in Yaft Abad.'

The doctor comes over, this time more confidently.

'You're not a woman, you're a lioness,' he whispers in my ear before going up to the window and creating a halo of condensation on it as he says to the officer, '*Beloved of my heart*, I'm all ears. What seems to be the problem?'

'Like I said, the passport's still in Yaft Abad.'

I nudge Dâryoush aside and, keeping my face away from

the condensation left by his breath, I maintain a note of authority in my voice as I ask the officer, 'What should I do now?'

'I'm not the man to ask. The normal process takes a month. But if you're recommended by Colonel Azardel, one word from him can cut the waiting by a quarter. Next!'

Dâryoush inclines his head and sends him a kiss with the tips of his fingers.

'So? What should I do now?' I ask helplessly.

'I haven't a clue. First we need to give Colonel Azardel time to grieve. Then we have to sort out your *kart-e melli*. And finally we've got to send you for a blood test.'

Which, in plain speaking, means: I can't help you any more.

I call my aunt over. Her face is daubed with flour.

'Is that it then? Have you got your passport?' she asks, wiping her face.

'No, I'll explain later.'

'She'll get it, she'll get it,' says Dâryoush to reassure her. 'But she's such a pessimist! And neurotic! You can see she's lived abroad and read Schopenhauer.'

'Do you know Schopenhauer?' I ask, amazed.

'Ah, you thought your doctor was uneducated, did you? Schopenhauer was born in Danzig in 1788 and died on the 21st of September 1860 at Frankfurt am Main. Who can say fairer than that?'

I'm blown away. A whole new world is opening up before my feet. What's Schopenhauer got to do with all this? I expected anything, but not him.

Dâryoush takes a piece of paper from his pocket and unfolds it.

'Do you want a quote from him? Listen to this: "Man's

life swings, like a pendulum, between pain and boredom."
If you like, after the *kart-e melli* and the blood test, I can
take you to the library at the University of Law where
they've got Schopenhauer's complete works.'

'*Badan, badan*, later.'

As we leave the building and cross the courtyard
Dâryoush suddenly stops.

'You really had me going earlier. What a nerve! I mean,
really well done! And there I was thinking you were so
fragile and depressive . . . I tell you, anyone else would
have snapped.'

'Snapped because of what?' asks my aunt, who doesn't
know what's going on.

'The officer told her she was banned from leaving the
country,' Dâryoush tells her.

'You're banned from leaving?' she asks, horrified.

'No, he just said it to get rid of me, to put me in a state,
to force me to put up a fight for a week and then, in the
end, to tell me my passport was all OK after all.'

Dâryoush is still holding his page of quotes, and chooses
another one which he reads out: 'What each of us seeks
out and loves above anything else, not only in simple conversation but even more so in public service, is the
inferiority of other individuals.'

'Schopenhauer?'

'Schopenhauer,' he confirms.

My aunt and I go through the booth for checking
women's clothes.

'Your application hasn't been sorted out, has it?' the
inspector asks.

'No.'

'See you soon then.'

'See you soon.'

We leave and I still can't work out how she recognised me earlier from amongst thousands of visitors, or how she knew just then that I had been unsuccessful.

Dâryoush is waiting for us outside, beside his van. I thank him and he says I shouldn't be too worried. I give a little nod of agreement and he gets into his van and leaves, without putting his seat belt on.

I won't see him again.

My aunt and I get into the *ajans* which is waiting for us. The steward asks where we're going and we tell him although we know he won't be able to take us there. After a hundred 'lefts', 'rights' and 'straight ons' we're finally back outside my aunt's building. When the time comes to pay, the usual *tarof* rituals begin.

'How much do I owe you?'

'Nothing, you're my guests, please.'

'That's very kind, but how much to I owe you?'

Before we get out the steward says, 'I wouldn't want to put you in an awkward situation but you didn't happen to forget to pick up a passport form for me, did you?'

I feel like telling him it's all Schopenhauer's fault.

'I'm bound to have to go back there in a few days' time. I promise I'll ask for the form next time. It just wasn't possible today.'

He gives me his card which has a picture of a pair of glasses shaped like the windows on an aeroplane, with his name and mobile number each written on one of the 'lenses'.

We go our separate ways, and for a few moments I worry about how he's going to find his way home, then forget him.

In the lift my aunt and I decide we won't disclose our failure to my uncle. It might set back his recovery. We're greeted by Samira, Masserat, Hamid, Mohtaram and Kiara. My uncle sits up in bed in one agile move (the whole question of my passport has fascinated him from the start) and asks, 'Have you got your passport? Let me see it.'

I explain that I need to wait a few more days.

'Did you speak to that man about me?' he asks.

My aunt goes and sits down on the edge of his bed and describes our morning in detail starting with the driver who was a steward on internal flights, then the inspector who remembered my blood pressure problems, the exotic juice that Iran exports like nowhere else, the cream puffs she couldn't resist and finally Schopenhauer, the major German philosopher whose complete works can be found in the library of Tehran's University of Law.

My uncle listens patiently.

'I can make myself understood in Persian, can't I?' he says. 'In amongst all this, did you talk to the man about me?'

I leave the living room to take refuge in my aunt's bedroom and call my husband, Nargess, the photographers and why not the bird-catcher, the one who said he knew every lieutenant at the passport office in Yafi Abad?

I start with my husband, but get the answering machine and don't leave a message. What could I tell him? Then I call Nargess and she answers very quietly, saying she's right in the middle of a funeral ceremony. I can actually hear passages from the Koran in Arabic around her. I don't press the point. I hang up.

Then I dial the number for the two photographers.

'Hello, Ecbatana studios, can I help you,' Morad's voice says.

'Hello, *agha* Morad, it's Nahal Tajadod.'

'Oh, hello, how are you?'

'I'm very well thank you. And you?'

'I'm still expecting your daughter to come for her portrait. She needs to wear a brightly coloured dress, a ribbon in her hair and pearl earrings.'

'*Agha* Morad, I'm not calling about that. I've just been with Dr Askarnia at the Central Passport Office where we were told my passport was still in Yaft Abad.'

'So?'

'I don't know what to do next, to be honest. We've waited a week and nothing's happened.'

'I see. You know it wouldn't have come to this if the results of the autopsy had been different. But don't get yourself in a state. I'll call the doctor straight away.'

I'm tempted, I have to say, to get in touch with the bird-catcher. But, warned off by my little voice, I resist the urge to launch myself into a world where the fate of my passport might be decided between a parrot and a canary.

For a while I abandon my administrative worries. I need to go and see an old puppeteer to invite him to Montpellier in June for the *Printemps des comédiens*, a festival my husband runs. The traffic ban is lifted at five in the afternoon and Hashem's registration number ends in an even number (which means he can travel on Saturdays, Mondays and Wednesdays) so I could get him to drive me there today, Saturday, at half-past five.

I take my daughter with me and warn everyone we could be back very late because the puppeteer's house is a long way away in the Sar Tcheshmeh quarter. Even though she doesn't like being out after dark, my aunt immediately suggests coming with us. I know why she's suddenly decided to do this: Sar Tcheshmeh is where she spent her childhood.

All through the journey my aunt tells me about her grand-mother who (how many times have I heard this?) was convinced there was treasure hidden in their house.

'One day, when I was about five or six,' she explains, 'they called in a diviner who measured every nook and cranny of the house with a surveyor's compass, drew up scale plans and recited all sorts of prayers before pointing to the cellar door and saying, "Dig here, you'll find a crypt and in that crypt is the Assassins' hidden treasure. But beware, this must only be done by the hands of a blonde-haired girl child from this family."'

'What treasure?' Kiara asks.

'The Assassins' treasure,' I tell her, thinking she can't be getting too bored in Iran: yesterday she visited the queen's bedroom, then met a thief and today she's discovering buried treasure. How could you improve on that?

Hashem, who can't wait to launch into his litany of English words, tries to bring an end to my aunt's remi-niscing by intervening, 'blonde hair! you won't find that in families like ours!'

'When I was little I was fair,' my aunt says. 'My grand-mother summoned me and showed me to the diviner. But he immediately decreed that the girl who would open the Assassins' treasure had to have not just fair hair, put prop-erly blonde.'

'But you don't get blondes in our families!' Hashem says again.

'No, but I really wanted to go into the crypt and find the treasure,' my aunt goes on. 'I was barely older than Kiara, you know. So I asked the diviner, "And what if I do open it? what would happen then?" and he said grimly, "Seven years' bad luck." The next day my grandmother had the cellar door walled up.'

'And what if I open it?' Kiara asks.

'You're not blonde either. But when, much later, after we'd moved out of that house, your aunt was born with beautiful blonde curls, your grandmother and I remembered the old diviner's prediction.'

'Go on. Then what? then what?' Kiara asks.

'And then we forgot.'

'Please, let's open the treasure,' she begs.

'Well, to start with let's go and see some puppets, OK?' I say.

Kiara nods. Before the treasure, some puppets. We park outside the Sar Tcheshmeh area, a labyrinth of narrow streets inaccessible by car. We ask a few locals who all know the puppeteer and are happy to take us to him. In keeping with the *tarof*, I decline. But Hashem eventually asks a teenager to take us there.

'That's our house, there, look!' my aunt exclaims suddenly. 'That's definitely it.'

The teenager tells us we're there and rings the bell of the house opposite. I hardly have time even to glance at the front door of what was my mother's family home, framed by two benches carved into the walls and with two ancient lanterns towering above it. The puppeteer Mr Fayaz comes to the door to greet us in person. He's a very fine-looking elderly man. He could play the part of the kindly grandfather in any number of television series.

'*Bonjour*,' he says in French to Kiara, 'how are you, sweetheart?'

His French has no accent at all. It doesn't seem right to ask him straight out how he speaks such impeccable

French, so I introduce the teenager to him. 'This young man was kind enough to show us where you live.'

'Well, he's very welcome,' announces our host.

The teenager follows us inside quite naturally.

We all go into a small garden with an ornamental basin in the middle of it where water spouts from a carved lion's head. Pots of jasmine dotted along the walls give off their heady fragrance. The house dates back to the nineteenth century, a rarity in Iran, a country where everything is pulled down to make way for the new, which will in turn be pulled down. A few steps lead up to a terrace and the hall. We take off our shoes and go up the steps. The teenager, our guide, does the same.

'You have to take your shoes off like at school,' Kiara points out.

The puppeteer invites us into the living room which opens on to the terrace through french windows with stained-glass panes. We sit directly on the floor, leaning on carpet-covered cushions – a haven of well-being. A young woman in a light-coloured chador serves us tea.

'This is my daughter-in-law. She paints miniatures.'

She has a beauty reminiscent of images from Persian poetry: swooning eyes, arched eyebrows and slender pursed lips. Our host waves at the paintings on the walls and announces proudly, 'Her work.'

I get up and look at one of the pictures at random: a woman playing the mandolin. Then a girl comes in and offers us a tray of pastries. We are told she is the daughter of the house and a virtuoso on the *setar*, a long-necked lute. She's wearing the red tunic and sequined scarf of Turkmen tribes and has such a typically Persian kind of beauty she could grace the front cover of a tourist guide to Iran.

The miniaturist and the musician sit on either side of my aunt and myself.

'Is the treasure here?' Kiara asks.

'No. Remember, we're going to see puppets here.'

Still, she goes down into the garden in search of treasure. As I get up to follow her one of the young women, the musician, reassures me, 'My brother will keep an eye on her. He's out in the garden.'

The girls insist we help ourselves to *zaboun*. Forgetting this morning's cream puffs, my aunt takes one of these cakes.

'It tastes just like they did when I was ten years old,' she says.

I can't help thinking of Proust's *madeleine*.

'Is the Shokoufeh pâtisserie still here?' my aunt asks.

'Do you know it?'

'I spent the first twelve years of my life in the house opposite.'

'In the goldsmith's workshop?' the musician asks.

My aunt and I look at each other in amazement.

The puppeteer gets up and opens one of the french windows.

'See for yourself,' he says.

On the far side of the street we can see the wall of the other house, its shuttered windows, a few plane trees and a tall chimney stack which seems to be in use.

The teenager steps forward and says, 'We don't know anything about those people. No one's ever seen them. When there's smoke coming from the chimney that means they're there, they're working.'

Just then Kiara comes running in followed by the puppeteer's son, as devastatingly good-looking as the legendary Joseph. I remember the episode in Joseph's history when his sudden arrival in the harem so flustered the women, who were busy peeling oranges, that they cut their hands because they couldn't take their eyes off his face. I'm saved, I'm not peeling any oranges!

'Why's no one ever seen them?' Kiara wonders.

The puppeteer's son says hello to us and adds, 'Because they're cursed.'

'What's cursed?'

The doorbell rings and the puppeteer goes out to greet the Director of the Theatres Association who has come to see him.

'My brother is a calligrapher,' says the musician, pointing to a wall decorated with calligraphy.

The puppeteer comes back into the living room with the high-ranking official. The latter sports the full beard of official representatives, the Chairman Mao collar and the characteristic parting on the far left-hand side of his head. I never knew what this particular hairstyle was for until a friend told me: combing one's hair before praying is considered a beneficial sign of piety. So, in order to imply that they spend their time praying, fanatics carefully mark out this distinctive parting. Another sign.

Despite his Islamic dress, the man looks me in the eye and smiles at me within a couple of sentences. I think to myself that if he were put in an Arab turban he would look like the idealised effigies of the Imam Ali, the Prophet's son-in-law.

We eventually sit down opposite the elderly Mr Fayaz. He reaches for a box made of inlaid wood and delicately takes out two figurines: a young man with kohl-lined eyes, wearing a turquoise silk tunic over scarlet leggings and well-polished boots, and a young woman with blonde hair and a face made of porcelain, wearing a long mauve velvet dress. Mr Fayaz slips his hand inside the costume of the hero, Amir Araslan (a figure familiar to everyone) and starts animating the puppet. Amir Araslan moves up and down and announces his immediate departure for foreign lands. I can't help myself thinking about his passport.

In the blink of an eye Amir Araslan arrives in *Farang*, in other words France, where he meets Farokh Lagha, the king's daughter. The two characters draw together, then flee, call each other, then argue – all before Kiara's fascinated eyes.

My telephone rings and I see it's my husband calling from Paris. I get up and apologise as the puppeteer interrupts his performance. I take a few steps back and, as usual, hear the same voice asking the same question, 'So, what news of your passport? Where have you got to with it?'

How can I tell him that Dâryoush (he doesn't know my contact looks like Dâryoush and doesn't actually know who Dâryoush is either) has fallen out with the colonel since revealing the results of tests from his cousin's autopsy, and therefore can't really help me any more? How can I explain all this over the phone in a half-whisper in a stranger's house?

'When are you coming home? Do you at least know that?'

'Soon, I hope. I just need to find someone high up at the Central Passport Office.'

'What about your colonel?'

'It didn't work.'

'Why?'

'Because he's in mourning, I'll explain.'

'But you will be here on Tuesday?'

'I can't promise anything, I haven't got anyone at the moment. It could take longer. Maybe a month.'

'A month?'

'I'll explain. Don't be angry with me. I'm really doing everything I can.'

I change the subject by telling my husband that right now I'm with Mr Fayaz, the most celebrated puppeteer in Iran, who lives in a typically Persian house surrounded by his children who are all more beautiful than each other and all of whom have some wonderful artistic talent. Mr Fayaz stands up, puts his hand to his chest as a sign of humility and asks whether he can speak to my husband. I hand him my mobile straight away and he starts talking in French, saying he would very much like to work with my husband on a puppet show inspired by *The Conference of Birds*.

All of a sudden a curvaceous woman in a scarf and suit comes into the room and apologises for being late.

'My lesson ended an hour and a half ago and I've only just got here. I hope you've been well taken care of,' she adds with some concern.

She is the mistress of the house and I assure her that we've been made very welcome in her absence. The puppeteer puts his hand over the mobile, gestures to my aunt and tells his wife that she lived in the house opposite as a child.

'So could you have known each other?' his wife asks.

'Our mothers were friends,' he says. 'Hers died very young, may God have mercy on her, and they left.'

I avoid looking at my aunt: I'm sure she's crying.

The old puppeteer, sensing an awkward pause, a sadness, carries on, 'My wife is late because she's just got back from her Koran lesson. She teaches the Koran to a group of young women.'

Instantly I feel a longing to learn the Koran with her, in this house where a youthful Joseph practises calligraphy,

where a young woman's swooning eyes pore over unfin-
ished miniatures, where the very emissary of Persian
beauty plays the *setar*, where the host – who speaks excel-
lent French – is planning to work on a French adaptation
of Attar's play, and where an official dignitary looks like
Imam Ali and dares to look a woman in the eye and smile
at her.

Everything would be so simple, I think. Everything
would be so wonderful.

I suggest my aunt should sign up for Mrs Fayaz's lessons.
She pinches my hand to stop me.

The moment the puppeteer has said goodbye to my
husband and hung up the phone he asks, 'Are you having
trouble with a passport?'

I start off with a *tarof*: 'No, it's nothing, it'll sort itself
out.'

My aunt pinches me again to encourage me to accept
potential help. She's right: we're in the presence of a government official, someone in a real position of authority. I
tell them briefly about my misadventures and how I'm
imminently meant to be giving a conference in Paris about
the links between Sufism and Buddhism.

'Oh, I would so love to attend that conference!' sighs
the puppeteer.

I promise to send him a transcript. 'Joseph' writes their
email address on a piece of paper and hands it to me.

The Director of the Theatres Association swiftly takes
his mobile from his pocket, calls someone and tells them
calmly but firmly, 'Tomorrow morning I would like you to
accompany Mrs Tajadod to the Central Passport Office. I'll
put her on. She'll tell you what it's about.'

I don't mention Dâryoush, the colonel's cousin's body
or false alarms concerning Section 1. I keep all that to myself.

'My passport's been stuck in Yaft Abad for a week and I need to leave on Tuesday,' I say simply.

'In Yaft Abad? Why Yaft Abad?' asks a man's voice, sounding very surprised.

'I, shall we say, knew someone there. But he wasn't able to do anything.'

'Meet me at ten o'clock tomorrow outside the Central Passport Office.'

'I'm sorry but how will I recognise you?'

Hope has just blossomed again. At the same time I remind myself that while I'm there tomorrow I must pick up a form for the steward, the one who drives an *ajans* but isn't a taxi driver.

'I'll recognise you,' replies the voice.

My daughter launches herself at the official's mobile and begs him to show her his pictures. He agrees and, before my eyes, promptly starts running through pictures of President Khatami, the Head of Parliament and his own wife, her hair duly hidden under a scarf. In a split second Kiara takes my mobile from my handbag and, before I have time to stop her, presses the photo gallery button, showing off my pictures: in a bikini beside a river in the Hérault region or sitting at the table cheerfully clinking wine glasses with my husband. For a moment I think my meeting the next day is likely to be cancelled and I may have to contact the bird-catcher.

Just then a young man rushes into the room, out of breath and carrying a copy of the Persian translation of Luis Buñuel's *My Last Sigh*.

As he sits down Mr Fayaz says, 'This is my eldest son, he's a filmmaker.'

My aunt pinches me yet again: she's worried I'll strike up a conversation with the young filmmaker. If we get on

to the subject of Buñuel, with whom my husband worked
for twenty years, we'll be here all night. My aunt's worried
about my uncle, we ought to be leaving. I promise the
puppeteer I'll see him in Montpellier, secretly hoping the
whole family might be able to come.

The official takes Kiara in his arms.

'I've got a boy of seven. Your daughter can be my
daughter-in-law,' he announces.

Everyone hopes so. '*Inshallah.*'

I don't say that I might have other dreams for her. But
I'm delighted to see he doesn't mind about my obvious
sins: bikinis and wine.

We thank each member of the family and leave. Once
outside, my aunt stops on the doorstep of her old house. I
stand beside her, holding my daughter's hand. The official,
Hashem and the teenager are all standing behind us. My
aunt reaches out and touches one of the padlocks, the one
shaped like a lamb and meant to be used by women. She
turns it and the door springs open. The teenager comes
closer and encourages us to go in.

'Go on!' he says. 'That's the first time I've seen this
door open.'

'But this isn't our house. We need to let the owners
know,' I say.

The official takes a step forward and calls out, 'Hello? Is
anyone there?'

My aunt, who hasn't said a word, suddenly closes the
door.

'Let's go!' she says. 'It's getting dark. We're late.'

'If you ever want to visit this house,' the official offers, 'I
could arrange it for you through my colleagues at the
Heritage Department.'

'Thank you so much. *Badan, badan*, later.'

When we come out of the old quarter the director gets into his official car and we head over to Hashem's. Before leaving us the teenager asks my aunt, 'How did you manage to open that door?'

'Three turns to the right and one to the left. It hasn't changed in sixty years.'

No one speaks on the way home. For once even Hashem respects our silence and Kiara falls asleep on my knee.

When we arrive Hashem drives down into the car park while my aunt, Kiara and I take the lift. Once inside, as usual, we simultaneously take off our scarves.

'Why didn't you go into the house?' I ask my aunt casually.

'There were three of us on that doorstep: Kiara, you and me. And my sister, my mother and my grandmother were inside. I saw all three of them, at the ages we are today.'

Her sister (who was my mother), her mother and grandmother are all dead. That was why she shut the door.

Sunday

My aunt wakes me at about eight o'clock in the morning by calling and asking, 'The things I saw and heard yesterday . . . just tell me, was that part of my dreams or real life?'

Like all Iranians, in key moments I can express myself by quoting our great poets. Most of my compatriots quote Hafez but my mother taught me to refer to Roumi whom she saw as the supreme master.

I reply to my aunt's question with these words (which she knows as well as I do): 'That transparent state is like the moment you embark on sleep, when you leave who you are to go into yourself, when you can hear yourself and yet believe that someone else has revealed a secret to you. There is no boundary between sleep and wakefulness.'

She says the closing words along with me and then goes straight on to say, 'Don't forget to take a little present for the inspector woman.'

Kiara, Mohtaram and Hashem are already preparing to go to my aunt's house as they do every day. Hashem offers to drop me off again.

'You still haven't got it,' Mohtaram reminds her husband.

'There's not only the limited traffic ban but also the whole system of odd and even numbers. It's Sunday today, and you can only go as far as ASP.'

She calls an *ajans* for me, and I take two tins of coffee for the inspector at the Central Passport Office before going downstairs. As I pass Mr Eskandari he watches me sympathetically.

'How many times have they made you go backwards and forwards!' he exclaims.

The driver today is neither Gheysar, nor the one who makes you overpay him, nor the steward in need of a form to get out, but a calm man in his seventies with a white moustache, wearing a blue shirt buttoned up to the neck. The assumed portrait of Imam Ali hangs from the rearview mirror of his car, an old Peykan. As I look at it I can confirm that the Director of the Theatres Association whom I met yesterday really does look like the 'Lion of God', Imam Ali.

In the car I call Nargess and tell her how impatient my husband is and about meeting a high-ranking official from the Department of Culture who has promised to sort everything out.

'He'll do it. He'll do it. And don't forget this evening we're meant to be going to the opening night of that painter who works on the corpses.'

'What corpses?'

'The ones from the earthquake in Bam. I'll come and pick you up. You're on my way.'

I know I'm not on her way this time either but she'll do it anyway.

'Excuse me, madam,' the driver with the white moustache then says. 'I'm taking the liberty of giving you a couple of pieces of advice because I'm old enough to be your father.'

What would be the point of telling him my father was born in 1886? The conversation could go right on till Tuesday and stop me getting home to Paris.

'"Oh God, grant that my friend comes home in good health and delivers me from the chains of reproachfulness." Those are Hafez's words, madam. You mustn't get upset if the *yar*, your friend or husband, is impatient with you.'

'I'm not the one getting upset, he is.'

'On that subject Hafez says, "The violence of those close to us is goodness and generosity."'

So Hafez is along for the ride this morning. In Tehran we're never alone: we have our poets as companions, friends, parents.

When I get out, as always, I ask the driver to wait for me. How is the man from the Theatres Association going to recognise me, I wonder. I look at shop windows: sports equipment, Adidas shoes (and to think I forgot the papers meant for Gérard Depardieu at that show laid on by the decorator who specialised in Asian-ethnic interiors!), T-shirts, electrical goods, cuddly toys. I go into the last shop but my little voice immediately warns me off buying a Mickey Mouse and going into administrative premises with an American rodent.

As I walk out a man comes up to me.

'Mrs Tajadod?'

'Yes, hello.'

It's the man I'm waiting for. He introduces himself. He is about sixty with long greying hair and round-rimmed glasses. He could quite easily be a John Lennon who escaped assassination. He is holding a large gift-wrapped parcel.

'It's a pressure cooker,' he says.

'Really?'

'Yes. It is for the employee who went to Yaft Abad at seven o'clock this morning to pick up your passport.'

I quickly deduce that I need to pay him back for the pressure cooker and even add a little something to cover travelling expenses for the man in question. Why should the Theatres Association finance this trip, after all?

'Would you be so kind as to let me contribute to the cost?' I say.

'Of course not, are you mad? Pressure cookers, food processors, mini sewing-machines – these are our bread and butter, everyday things.'

We each head to our designated inspection areas. I go into the booth for women and say hello to the inspectors. The one who recognised me yesterday says, 'You were right not to bring your mother back. They find places like this tiring.'

I automatically open my handbag but she waves at me to close it. I give them each a tin of coffee.

'A little something from Paris.'

'What is it?'

'Coffee.'

'French coffee?' asks the one I recognise, as she gesticulates to another visitor to remove her lipstick.

'Yes, it's from Paris.'

'It's not Turkish coffee then?' the other woman points out.

'No, it tastes different.'

'Tuck that blonde hair inside your scarf,' she orders a new arrival, then turns back to me: 'and how do you make it?'

I suddenly realise they must have neither electric percolators nor cafetières. Should I go out and stock up on cafetières in the shop next door? My little voice forbids it.

'One spoonful of coffee per person and per cup,' I say quickly before leaving.

I meet up with John Lennon in the inner courtyard and he points to an office on the left.

'You need to start there. You need to queue in the corridor like everyone else. I'll stand to one side. When it's your turn you go in and show your letter of introduction to the lieutenant, a filthy-tempered man. Whatever you say, don't tell him you've got anyone here with you.'

He leaves me in the corridor and disappears. There are twenty people waiting in front of me. I feel like calling someone for help, but there isn't anyone left: Colonel Azardel has fallen out with Dâryoush and even the bird-catcher wouldn't be able to do anything for me now. My passport has left the office in Yaft Abad in exchange for a pressure cooker.

Quite soon it's my turn because the filthy-tempered lieutenant doesn't grant anyone more than a couple of minutes. I walk up to his desk and he doesn't look up. I hand him the letter of introduction which he reads quickly and hands back to me, still without looking up.

'*Madar*, mother,' he says, 'come back in a week.'

I want to protest but I'm pinioned by that *madar*. It's the first time I've been called that. I leave his desk older, defeated, stooped, part of a different generation, and find John Lennon sitting on the stairs.

'What did he say?' he asks.

I feel like telling him he called me *madar* but restrain myself.

'Nothing. He read the letter and told me to come back in a week.'

'Perfect. Now we can attack.'

I don't understand what he's so happy about. I'm still in shock from the *madar*.

'Meanwhile,' he says, 'I've given the pressure cooker to its recipient and got your passport. But I wasn't allowed to hold on to it so I've handed it to the authorities and now you can claim it through the official channels.'

We go into the ground-floor concourse and John Lennon indicates one of the counters to me.

'Sit yourself down there. I'm going to call my contact. He'll come and check the information on the computer and then, if everything's OK, he'll give you your new passport. Don't talk to him too much. All right?'

'All right.'

I sit down and an officer arrives, passport in hand. As predicted, he consults his computer and then leaves. I haven't exchanged a single word with him. I look round for John Lennon: he's leaning on a long counter, drinking fruit juice. I go over to join him and he offers me some 'exotic' juice, regurgitating Dâryoush's sentence word for word, 'Do you know, all of Europe's addicted to products made by this Iranian brand.'

'I know, I've had it before.'

'Did you also know that Mon Chéri liqueur chocolates are made here?'

'No, I didn't.'

'They are, they are, I promise you. I got that from a trusted source.'

'I believe you. But I just wanted to let you know that the officer didn't give me my passport.'

'Perfect.'

Why is he pleased with that? Why is everything so perfect? I still can't see it.

'You didn't speak to him, did you?' he adds, offering me the exotic juice.

'No, not a word.'

'Perfect.'

He goes out and I see him call someone on his mobile. As I finish my juice I simmer at the thought that he got one over on me with the Mon Chéri chocolates being made in Iran. If he fails with my passport I'll tell him I can guarantee it would be impossible for an Islamic country to agree to produce liqueurs on its own territory. No question about it.

Out of the blue I hear my name being called from the far end of the room on the public address system: 'Tajadod, counter number 5!'

I don't know what to do. I go to find John Lennon and he waves me over to the counter. When I get there the officer checks my name and hands me a passport. I take it and open it: it really is mine.

The passport problem has just been resolved.

John Lennon and I walk back across the courtyard and I thank him, taking care not to throw any doubt on his revelations about Mon Chéri. I go into the women's inspection booth.

'At last! I've got my passport,' I say.

'When are you leaving?'

'The day after tomorrow.'

'A piece of advice: go and never come back,' says the one I'm getting to know. Then she stands up and recites in my ear the prayer for those who are leaving: '*Fallah-o khey-ron hafezan va hova arham-o rahemin.*'

I kiss her and her colleague, and leave the Central Passport Office with tears in my eyes. I'm filled with a sense of triumph: through my own contacts I've succeeded in cutting the waiting time by three weeks. I tell myself I can achieve anything now, changing the braiding on my chairs, not getting into a taxi with a positively horizontal driver, reclaiming my confiscated land . . .

I offer to drop John Lennon off and he agrees so we get into the *ajans* together.

'*Are you a lion or a fox?* Did you win or lose?' asks the driver.

'It's done, it's sorted.'

'That's why Hafez says, "Divine grace exercises its power, the messenger angel brings good news."'

My blood pressure drops abruptly and I'm annoyed with myself for not bringing any chocolate or dried fruit with me. John Lennon gives the driver the address for the Theatres Association before suddenly asking me, 'How's Peter?'

'Peter?'

'Yes, Peter, Peter Brook.'

I tell him he's fine while I struggle to find a connection between Peter Brook and John Lennon.

'And Wilson? And Stockhausen? And Merce Cunningham?'

'They're all very well, as far as I know.'

'Nahal *khanoum*, do you know how I know them all? Because in the days of the Shiraz festival I was already in charge of all the paperwork. I knew them all, quite well.'

The period he's referring to lasted about ten years, from 1966 to 1976. There was a major arts festival in Shiraz every year. My mother, whose plays were performed there, took me as often as possible. It was there that, aged about twelve, my best friend and I discovered different kinds of theatre, *katakali, no, qawwali*, electro-acoustic music, 'poor' theatre, contemporary dance, Grotowski, Kantor, Terayama . . .

Later, when I moved to Paris, I felt I'd already seen everything. France was just discovering Bob Wilson while the Iranian that I was had seen many hours of his production *KA MOUNTAIN and GARDENIA TERRACE* (the one that went on for seven days and seven nights), sitting wrapped in my mother's shawl at Haft Tan in Shiraz.

The ten years John Lennon is talking about were a golden era in my life, a time when everything was as it should be, when the land in Mazandaran still belonged to us, my mother wrote, painted and sang, my father was working on the definitive catalogue of ninth-century works, my aunt and uncle drove round a Tehran of three million inhabitants in a white Thunderbird, the dead were buried back in their native soil, and the Revolution hadn't happened.

'In fact, now that I know you a little better, I can finally tell you how very sorry I was when your mother died.'

This is too much. I think I'm going to snap.

'When I told people in the office I was going to see you today, all of them – old and young – sent their regards. They really would love it if you came up and had a glass of tea.'

We have just reached the front door of the Theatres Association.

'*Badan, badan*, another time. There's nothing to keep me in Iran a moment longer now. Thanks to you, I'm leaving the day after tomorrow, and I haven't done anything yet.'

He takes my hand and holds it in his for a long time.

'Say hello to everyone, to all my old directors,' he says. 'Tell them we haven't forgotten them, tell them we owe them a great deal.'

He gets out and I watch him walk away. He turns round once and waves to me, then I lose sight of him. The driver, who has heard everything, quotes another verse from Hafez: 'The end of a time of sadness is upon us, *that* is finished and *this* shall finish too.'

The *ajans* drops me at my aunt's house and the *tarof* war breaks out between the driver and myself. He eventually gives in and I pay, not without Hafez's intervention: 'May the memory stay with me, the memory of someone who, when the time came to travel, neither mentioned me nor cheered my heart with a farewell.'

I go up into the apartment and, once I've been embraced by all the women in Mohtaram's family and greeted by all the men, I run over to my uncle to show off my passport. He puts on his glasses, reads the information in minute detail, flicks through all the pages and concludes, 'I told you all there wouldn't be a problem. Before any sort of undertaking all you have to do is consider *the heavy and the light*, the pros and cons, and then go about it intelligently.'

I don't know whether I ever did actually consider *the heavy and the light*. Nor for that matter whether I went about any part of this process intelligently. But one thing is absolutely clear: I've got my passport.

'Does that mean you're leaving tomorrow?' my aunt murmurs sadly.

Kiara, who is being taught the different positions for Islamic prayer by Hamid, runs over.

'Are we going home to Paris? Are we going to see my cats?' she exclaims.

'Couldn't you stay one more day?' asks my aunt. It reminds me of my mother who, the day before I was to leave, would always ask me to stay another twenty-four hours. Which I invariably did. Until she was the one who left.

'No, no, I want to go home to see Daddy,' retorts my daughter.

I call my husband and Nargess to tell them the good news. My husband seems satisfied at last, although he does still point out that he'll never understand this country.

'Actually, now it's all over, how much should I give Dâryoush?' I ask Nargess.

'Nothing, don't give him anything. Without the guy from the Theatres Association your passport would still be in the office at Yaft Abad.'

'Can't I still thank him? He did everything he could!'

'Yes, you call your Dâryoush. Until yesterday I had to go down on my knees to get you to call him, and now you're the one suggesting you should. If you want to so badly, go ahead and call your Dâryoush.'

I call him but he doesn't answer. I won't try again. Nargess is right, I've always had a problem with phone calls: if I really have to call someone but they are engaged or not answering, I think the fact I've tried is enough. I've gone through the motions and only rarely will I try again. What I really love is leaving a message for someone who's engaged or not there. Then I know I've done what I needed to do and, therefore, won't have to call again.

The whole family now knows about my administrative exploits, and it's not long before I have proof: another call from the cousin who also needs to renew her passport.

'Congratulations, well done you! You were really very clever.'

'Thank you.'

'By the way, your doctor friend still isn't answering his phone. I've tried a thousand times – nothing. Is he really a doctor or does he just wear a tie and get people to call him doctor?'

'He doesn't wear a tie.'

'Have you seen him again?'

'Yes, but it wasn't him who sorted this out for me.'

'Who was it then?'

'Someone from the Theatres Association.'

'Did you pay him?'

'No.'

'How come? In this place if you don't pay nothing happens.'

How can I explain about John Lennon's devotion? Where would I start: with nights at the Shiraz festival where Ravi Shankar sat beside Hafez's tomb and played by candlelight right through till dawn; where, at sunrise and after two thousand five hundred years' silence, an ancient Avestic sound emerged from the caves of Persepolis, urging all creatures to wake?

'It's true, though. I didn't pay.'

'You've made me waste a whole week with your so-called doctor. Now, please be nice, call this man and ask him to help me. Unless you're not prepared to help me.'

'I'm sorry. I don't think it would be possible.'

'Oh well, have a good trip back, then.'

She hangs up and sours my sense of victory. I resent my aunt for calling from the rooftops about my new passport.

'It wasn't me, it was Hamid,' she says defensively.

My uncle sits up and says firmly, 'Come on, do the others keep us up to date on who all their contacts might be?'

He brings two pinched fingers up to his lips and zips them along his mouth, adding, 'My lips are sealed.'

'That's right, we only have to put the tip of a finger up our noses and all of Tehran gets in a state,' says my aunt.

'You mustn't put your fingers up your nose,' my daughter chips in.

Nargess comes by to take me to the opening night of the Bam corpses. I say goodbye to my aunt, uncle, daughter and all of Mohtaram's clan.

'Try and spend these last few hours with us,' my aunt suggests sadly.

I go out, smarting from my cousin's lack of understanding and my aunt's comment. In the lift I realise that I
completely forgot to get a passport form for the steward-
taxi-driver. I also remember my absent-mindedness in
giving the inspectors a present they will never be able to
use. Not forgetting my negligence in losing the market
report about introducing Adidas to Iran. And I didn't keep
my promise to reward the policeman at the office in Yaft
Abad with a fan. And . . .

'Come on, let's see this passport,' says Nargess, clearing
the passenger seat of her anti-theft lock and some skirts in
plastic sleeves back from the dry cleaners. I get into the car
and show off my trophy. She looks at my photograph and
seems satisfied.

'I finally went back to the music shop and exchanged
the Delkash boxed set. And I bought this too. Listen.'

She puts on a CD by Fereydoun Foroughi, the singer of
my teenage years. In a flash I'm fourteen again, I'm in the
living room at a friend's house, the lights are out and I'm
in my boyfriend's arms. His beard (which is already quite
thick for his age) scratches my neck and he sings a couple
of lines: 'Your body is like the midday sun in summer.' His
breath smells of vodka. My hands are in his hair, his are
inside my clothes. He is the most amazing boy at school –
the French *lycée* in Tehran, one of the very few mixed
schools. He's a revolutionary, Che Guevara style. At
school he wears military parkas like his idol, right through
to the summer holidays, up until the scalding heat of the
Tehran summer. All the girls, even at the top of the
school, fawn on him. In class when he deigns to reply to
a teacher's question in between two defiantly hand-rolled
joints, it's only ever to impress the teacher, to go effort-
lessly beyond some answer written in teaching manuals

and learned the night before. In his parka pockets, apart
from cigarette stubs, there are always a couple of novels.
He sits at the back of the classroom next to an obtuse
beefcake who's doing the same year for the third time. My
boyfriend has no school books or exercise books or pens.
He comes to school as other people would go to a café.
He sits down and buries himself in his books while the
teacher nervously covers the blackboard with mathemat-
ical equations. If he's ever disturbed and asked a question
he goes nonchalantly up to the blackboard and, just as
nonchalantly, completes the maths teacher's demonstration.

Meanwhile the girls have had time to note down the
title of his book. At break the next day they're all scattered
in isolation – on a bench, on the lawn in the large garden
or sitting on the stairs – so they can read their idol's chosen
book alone. We've been together for a year. His mother
died when he was thirteen and a half, my father six months
later. From our grief we created a relationship.

'*Yavash*, slow down, slow down, let me through!'
Nargess hurls at another driver. Then she strokes the steering wheel of her (Iranian-built) Peugeot 607 and adds,
'This car changed my life. When I'm stuck in traffic I put
on the air conditioning and a CD, and cut myself off from
the outside world. To think for thirty whole years I drove
my father's old Toyota with the windows wound down,
breathing in tons of carbon dioxide and sweating buckets!
What a waste!'

I leave my long-lost boyfriend's arms. He slips a note
between my breasts, which he thinks blossomed in his
very hands (he knew me before, during and after their
development). I pull it out and read: 'You are my dreams,
and my nightmares too.'

Nargess parks outside the gallery and puts the steering lock on. Everyone has these devices but hers manages somehow to be discreet and minimalist. I've sometimes seen drivers take a full fifteen minutes putting locks on the steering wheel, gearstick and clutch, and then checking the alarm and immobilisation systems.

The gallery is heaving with people and we can't get in. From inside we can hear Cigala singing to Bebo's piano accompaniment – an old Cuban pianist and the rising star of Andalusian song. I'm amazed at their simultaneous success in the Hispanic world and Iran.

'Yes, but it's because of the CD you gave me,' Nargess points out. 'Some friends came over to my apartment and cut a copy. A week later all of Tehran's swearing by Bebo and Cigala.'

I see my friend Davar coming towards us. As we are in a public place, we don't kiss.

'Have you got much further with the translation?' I ask as usual.

'I got stuck on the sentence: "*Nous sommes les propres juges, les bourreaux d'une justice qui règne ici-bas.*"'

Two young men with short hair, thin faces and glasses with thick lenses come up to us. They say hello to Davar and remind him that they met him at a book fair. Davar pretends to recognise them and introduces me to them. When they hear that I live in Paris they say almost in unison, 'To what extent would you say that Foucault and Deleuze commune with insanity?'

How to tell them I've read neither Foucault nor Deleuze, or hardly?

'Mr Malek,' they go on, 'how would you translate the word "rhizome", taken from Deleuze's vocabulary, into Persian?'

'In botany a rhizome is an underground stem,' Davar replies, 'like in bamboo.'

I move away, trying to avoid a conversation in which I could hardly fail to dishonour France. I stand on tiptoe to see inside: the crowd is dense and it looks impossible to get to the pictures. As usual, Nargess is surrounded by friends, artists and collectors. An interior designer friend in leather trousers, tinted glasses and orange Nikes suggests I should buy one of the painter's works – a dead woman's stiffened hands sticking out of the ground – and hang it in the hall of my apartment. I ask for time to think about it.

'You and your husband are both writers. It would be quite striking to come into your apartment and see a pair of hands there, straight away.'

'Yes but they're a dead woman's hands.'

'It would still be striking. Those hands reaching out . . . Very powerful.'

'Are you a writer?' a young woman – with an intact nose – asks.

'Yes.'

'What's your name?'

'Nahal Tajadod.'

'I've never read anything of yours.'

'I write in French.'

'In French?'

'Yes, I live there.'

'Do you think Woody Allen was really faithful to Derrida's ideas in *Deconstructing Harry*?'

Where have I landed? Perhaps I should hide behind Nargess's car so no one can make me admit I've neither read Derrida nor seen *Deconstructing Harry*.

News that all the paintings have been sold reaches us. The invisible creature that animates my little voice can breathe. The two of us have just avoided buying an image based on the muddied hands of a woman who lost her life in Bam.

Davar comes over with his two Deleuzians.

'We are deserts,' one of them quotes, 'but populated with tribes, fauna and flora. And all these populations, all these crowds, can do nothing to stop the desert, which is our very asceticism.'

I introduce them to the girl who specialises in 'deconstruction', and she adds, 'The process of deconstruction presupposes never truly freeing itself from whatever it demystifies: it works alongside existing concepts, plays on them so they play against each other, strives to *shift* oppositions without claiming to banish them.'

I would so like them to ask me about Bernard-Henri Lévy and Arielle Dombasle, but to no avail. The discussion between the men with the glasses and the girl with the full nose becomes increasingly involved. I do ask them what they do for a living, though.

'Students of agronomy,' the men in glasses reply.

'I'm a solicitor,' says the woman.

I should have covered up the fact that I'm a French writer.

'You really must try this juice!' calls my decorator friend with a glass of exotic fruit juice in his hand.

'I've had it before,' I say, remembering Dâryoush and John Lennon.

'Do you know Iran exports it?'

'I do. But what you don't know is that Mon Chéri liqueurs are made here.'

'That doesn't surprise me. Anything's possible here. You were wrong not to buy anything,' he adds.

'But I couldn't even get inside!' I tell him.

'Those two hands would have been sensational in your hallway! I could picture them so well!'

'They're still a dead woman's hands,' I say.

'It is organisms that die, not life,' one of the Deleuzians points out.

Monday

Second to last morning waking in Tehran. I try to pack my suitcase before carrying out the *khodahafezi* ritual, my farewells. To do this I absolutely have to call everyone I've met on this trip. If I miss anyone by mistake I risk subjecting myself to their contempt should I come across them by chance in the street in a year's time. They would turn their back on me and avoid my even seeing them. Given that I don't like using the telephone, the whole question of *khodahafezis* seems more serious and solemn to me than the business with the passport. But it's impossible to avoid.

I start with the photographers. Once I've got hold of Morad I thank him, along with his colleague Hassan, for all the trouble they went to for me. I take the opportunity to tell them the happy epilogue to the passport saga, and finally let them know I'm leaving.

'So soon? But that's not possible! I haven't even done Kiara's portrait.'

'*Badan, badan.* I'll be back in three months,' I say, even though I know I won't be back for a year. 'I'd be very grateful if you could say a big thank-you to Dr Askarnia because without him I couldn't be leaving tomorrow. I've called him but he never answers.'

'He only did his duty,' Morad replies.

His duty surely can't have consisted in spending a whole day at the passport office in Yaft Abad with me, cancelling his lecture at the University of Law, intervening on my behalf with a grieving colonel at a time when he himself was dissecting the man's cousin, coming back to the Central Passport Office distressed and demoralised, and offering me exotic fruit juice and cream puffs.

'Nahal *khanoum*, you've just broken my heart with news of your departure. And so unexpectedly like that. We won't let you go without coming to see you. Give us five minutes this afternoon.'

I feel like saying no, finding some excuse to make them change their minds. I could say, for example, that a French friend has only just arrived in town and obviously I must take her out, even today, even though it's the day before I leave. Saying you have a foreigner, a *kharedji*, to show round the city is an infallible excuse. No one can resist an argument which brings the country's honour and its legendary hospitality into play. Still, I do pass this by my little voice which, for once, says nothing and raises no objections to Morad and Hassan's visit.

'Come whenever you like. I'm here all afternoon,' I say instead of 'For goodness' sake don't bother. We've said everything we have to say to each other.'

'We'll come over this afternoon, without fail.'

'What are you going to do about the studio?' I ask on the off chance, still in the hope of dissuading them. 'You can't close it, surely?'

'I'll ask my brother to come over and keep an eye on it. Don't worry.'

I remember that, according to Dâryoush's description, his brother is a feature-perfect copy of Alain Delon and I imagine Rocco in person behind the counter at the Ecbatana studio.

'See you this afternoon, then.'

I hang up and pour myself some coffee. Then I wait a few minutes before tackling my second obligation: calling the Director of the Theatres Association and the puppeteer. They both offer to help arrange for me to see the house in Sar Tcheshmeh, and I say my goodbyes with the promise that I shall see them in Montpellier. I fill my coffee cup and my reserves of courage, and call the disgruntled, offended cousin. I get her English-language messaging service and leave a message saying goodbye. I know I should call her back later and tell her in person that I'm going. Lastly, I call Nargess and Davar – which is not a chore, far from it. They too will come over this afternoon.

I start packing my bags, thinking all the time of a variety of hiding places for the pots of caviare. I usually camouflage them inside sports socks then slip them into my trainers, but I know that this method of concealment can be picked up in baggage checks. Still, I take the risk.

I have lunch with Mohtaram, Hashem and Kiara. The couple are delighted at the thought of accompanying us to the airport early the next morning. After a month of employment Hashem finally feels useful. Mohtaram, who loves trips to the airport, is already ironing her favourite coat, the one with a diamanté butterfly on the front; she loves wearing it and tells anyone who happens to pass that it was a present from Nahal *khanoum*, bought in Paris. She doesn't know the coat came from the dirt-cheap shop Tati and was probably made in India.

I allow myself a long siesta before waking and, adopting a habit of my mother's, eating some fruit. I realise that, as I get older, I do everything like her: a siesta followed by fruit.

The videophone rings. Mohtaram answers and tells me Mr Eskandari would like to come up. I tidy my hair, put on some perfume and wait for the caretaker in the living room. He comes in with a box of almond cakes, a Kurdish speciality that I open and try straight away. He's just about to leave when his colleague informs us, again through the videophone, that the photographers from Ecbatana studio are downstairs. Mr Eskandari himself gives them permission to come up, then comes back into the living room and asks me yet again and in such a gentle voice to talk to them about finding his son who has gone missing in Sweden. I promise I will.

Hashem opens the door to them, considering that the arrival of three na mahrams requires his presence. This small man with his chihuahua's head looks ready to challenge them at any moment. He considers himself first in line amongst those who watch over me and take care of me.

To avoid the possibility of my offer of coffee being accepted, Mohtaram rushes into the living room and pre-empts this by saying tea will be ready at any moment. I immediately detect bitter disappointment on the faces of the new arrivals: they'll have to have tea, like everywhere else. So I ask Mohtaram firmly to make coffee after all.

I've barely given this order when Morad runs his hands through his hair at some length and Hassan straightens the gold chain he wears round his neck. I see these as signs of contentment. They even go so far as to kiss Mr Eskandari, who sits down on one of the chairs upholstered by the photographers' wives, saying, '*ba edjazeh*, with your permission.'

The photographers sit down too. The lovely smell of French coffee fills the whole apartment as Hashem serves it out carefully, along with the almond cakes.

'*Inshallah*, when are you going to Sweden?' Mr Eskandari asks the photographers.

Morad gulps down too hot a mouthful and replies, 'Actually, if it's not too much to ask Nahal *khanoum*, we now need an accommodation certificate from the French authorities.'

Hashem, who doesn't like me doing favours for anyone but members of his own family, intervenes rather curtly: 'Nahal *khanoum* has far too much to do. When she's in Paris she needs to focus on her work and her conferences which are attended by hundreds of people.'

I don't know where he got this – unfortunately erroneous – information.

'I sometimes wonder whether people don't abuse her extreme kindness,' he adds, still standing.

'No, really,' I eventually say, to avoid offending the photographers, 'I'd be delighted to get hold of an accommodation certificate for you.'

I can immediately see two afternoons wasted, one to buy a fiscal stamp at the revenue offices in the rue Saint-Lazare and the other bickering with a clerk at the council in the 9th *arrondissement*. I can picture myself trying to explain to her that I can't supply the three necessary pay slips for the simple reason that my husband is a writer and receives only royalties. The clerk is unmoved when I show her a tax notice for a fairly substantial sum and point out that no one out of work would have to pay that much in taxes. Nothing for it. She won't give in.

I even go so far as to show her bank statements, electricity bills and the deeds to our house, all in vain. I pinpoint the exact size of the house: nothing doing. The woman has stopped looking at me and calls to the next person in the queue. I turn round, perhaps hoping that, a little way away, over by the lifts, I might spot my precious Dâryoush or even John Lennon with his pressure cooker under his arm. All I see are a couple of women who have come to find out about a crèche or ask about some allowance or other. I feel like giving this pen-pusher a list of all the famous people I know, saying I had supper with the mayor himself the night before . . . but I don't. I gather up my papers and go home trying to think of another way of getting the essential certificate. That's what I can look forward to, I'm sure of it.

On reflection, Hashem reckons that granting the photographers an accommodation certificate wouldn't in any way hinder my continued efforts to pamper his own children. With a note of pride in his voice, he announces, 'Anyway, thanks to madam's standing abroad, it would only take her a couple of minutes!'

I don't let myself think about my two afternoons again; I know they're lost.

All of a sudden the door opens and my aunt comes in with Dr Bashiri. She doesn't need to ring to come up to my apartment. Everyone stands up and I do the introductions.

'These gentlemen own the Ecbatana studio,' I say, indicating Morad and Hassan.

'Nahal *khanoum*,' cries Dr Bashiri, revealing his white teeth, 'are you using us to make a film or what? Yes, you're making us play parts! You who are personally acquainted with professionals in this field, you come and ask me the price of ID photos?!'

Morad and Hassan catch each other's eye and instantly seem to gauge my embarrassment while I try to work out what I owe them.

Morad brushes his fringe aside with a flick of his hand. 'I don't know the going rate . . . But at the Ecbatana studio it's free for madam,' he says.

'*Agha* Morad,' my aunt joins in, 'would you be able to come to our apartment to do some pictures of my husband?'

'The gentleman is unable to walk,' Hashem points out.

'My husband is temporarily unable to walk,' my aunt corrects him, still convinced this nuance will exorcise the incurable infirmity.

'For Nahal *khanoum*, we would go to the depths of hell,' Morad declares.

Hassan closes his eyes: he is happy to make the trip.

'*Inshallah* you shall avoid hell,' adds Mr Eskandari. 'But, once in Sweden, don't forget my son.'

'Mr Eskandari, I'm sure *agha* Morad and Hassan *agha* will do their best to track him down,' I say with a smile at the photographers, who nod in unison.

'Eskandari *djoun*,' Morad does go on to say, though, 'beloved Eskandari, we're still a long way from Sweden. But as soon as madam has sent us the accommodation certificate . . .'

'Oh, don't start putting madam under pressure!' cries Hashem who has just appeared with another tray of coffee and more almond cakes. At the same time Dr Bashiri takes a brochure from his pocket and hands it to me.

'Here, don't forget this! It needs adding to the market analysis I gave you the other day. It's for the same person.' Out of discretion, or caution, the doctor doesn't name Gérard Depardieu. Who can say where that could lead the conversation?

I take the document and leaf through it to put my mind at rest.

'This is very good,' I manage. 'It's all in English.'

'Yes, I spent the whole weekend on it. I packed my wife and son off to my parents, switched off my mobile, put three or four dictionaries out on my desk and produced that file.'

Quite impossible to admit to him that I've lost the original document, and in spite of his strenuous insistence on how ultra-confidential the whole thing was.

'I'm sure this will work, I feel it in my heart,' says Dr Bashiri.

'With God's help,' someone adds, not even knowing what we are talking about.

Still hoping to see every member of Mohtaram's family shod in Adidas trainers, my aunt adds, 'and if it works *agha* Morad and Hassan *agha* can open a sports shop in Stockholm.'

'Are you in sports?' Morad then asks the doctor.

'No, no. There's been some confusion. *I shall never set foot outside my kilim.* I'm a physio and I'll die a physio,' the doctor replies rather awkwardly, probably afraid someone will try to steal his precious concept: introducing Adidas to Iran.

'Anyway, I can assure you you can count on Nahal *khanoum*!' exclaims Morad.

The telephone rings and Mohtaram comes in with the handset. It's the cousin trying to get her passport again.

'Do you still not want to ask the guy from the Theatres Association to help me?' she nags quite irritably.

'But he's just an administrator! He has to do what his bosses tell him! I don't see how I could ask him to do this.'

'It's not difficult: the same way you did for yourself!

Unless you don't want to help me. In that case, just say so straight out!'

Mohtaram has stayed in the living room to take the telephone back and she points to me and says, 'They won't give her a moment's peace. She's leaving tomorrow and people are asking for her help right up to the last minute.'

'And your invisible Dr Thingy,' goes on the cousin, 'couldn't you make a bit of an effort to get in touch with him? To talk to him yourself?'

She is obviously convinced I've given her a false number.

'Well, actually,' I say, 'I'm sitting looking at a very good friend of Dr Askarnia's. Here, have a word with *agha* Morad. You can tell him what you want.'

Morad takes the telephone and runs his hand through his hair (some things never change).

'At your service,' he says, 'how can I help you?'

I'm completely up to speed on my cousin's wishes. Morad listens for a moment then takes out his mobile and gives her a number which seems to be Dâryoush's.

'Say Morad gave you his number, no, what am I saying, tell him it was Nahal *khanoum* herself and explain your situation to him.' Then he puts his hand over the mouthpiece and says, 'If he's got it back together with the colonel it'll only take him a day to sort out your cousin's problem.'

'*Inshallah!*' Mohtaram adds. 'Then at least she'll leave madam in peace.'

I privately wish with all my heart that the conclusions of the colonel's cousin's autopsy have been cleared up, that they have been favourably modified . . . I mean what's death got to do with all this, after all?

Morad politely takes his leave of my cousin and hands the telephone back to me.

'Thank you, thank you so much for giving me the wrong number,' she says in a voice loaded with resentment.

'But his number's changed!'

'I don't know what sort of people you spend time with,' she says, switching to sarcasm, 'but a doctor who changes his number in the space of a week strikes me as pretty dubious.'

'You don't have to call him, you know.'

'If he still hasn't answered by this evening, I'll find some other way.'

Oh, I would so love to tell her that she should have 'found some other way' right from the start! How can I explain what I've been through? And all the embarrassment and anxiety I'm sparing her? But I don't say a word. I wish her the smoothest renewal process possible and hang up.

Suddenly I remember *agha* Madjid, the property developer I met by the gates of the Central Passport Office on the first day, and his frantic quest for an eye.

'By the way, *agha* Morad, do you know whether an acquaintance of Dr Askarnia's managed to get hold of what he needed?' I ask, discreetly pointing to my eye.

'The doctor's heart is full of kindness. If he can help someone he'll go so far as risking his own life. I know what you're talking about –' here he gives a little wink '– *thanks be to God*, the man didn't go home empty-handed.'

'Let's hope he can also sort out a problem for the lady you've just been talking to,' my aunt chips in.

'*Inshallah*,' adds Mr Eskandari before taking from his pocket a piece of paper folded in four (the same old one, still just as tired and crushed). He asks Morad to write down a series of improbable numbers.

'It's the last telephone number my son gave us. Perhaps you'll be able to trace him from it. What do you think?'

'What are you still hoping for?' Hashem asks him. 'That some line that was cut off ten years ago should miraculously be reconnected just because *agha* Morad wills it?'

'*Na baba*, not at all, not at all,' replies Mr Eskandari, his eyes trained on his old piece of paper. 'But, apart from this, what else have I got to give them?'

Morad keys the numbers into his mobile and says, '*beh rouy-e tcheshm*, I will see to it with my own eyes, it will be a pleasure, Eskandari *djoun*. I promise you. But before that Nahal *khanoum* needs to send us the accommodation certificates. Otherwise how are we to get to Sweden?'

Nargess suddenly appears in the living room. All the caretakers know her, and even their stand-ins do, so she sweeps upstairs glibly without needing the videophone. She has brought some Iranian prunes for my husband, who loves them. I thank her and introduce her to Hassan, the only person she doesn't know.

Mr Eskandari wants to leave but Nargess holds him back and says out of the blue, 'Wait, I'm looking for an apartment of about two hundred square metres for a friend. If you happen to find one for her you'll get a very good *shirini*, piece of cake.'

The lure of 'cake', a commission, makes Mr Eskandari sit straight back down. Nargess sits close to him on a sofa designed by my decorator friend – the same one who tried only yesterday to persuade me to buy two dead hands sticking out of a devastated landscape.

Hashem comes back with more coffee and almond cakes.

'You really must try these,' I tell Nargess. 'They're a Kurdish speciality Mr Eskandari gave me.'

Nargess never refuses food. If ever I travel with her by car she can't get through more than half an hour without suggesting a clementine, some cucumber, a banana, sugared almonds, a bar of chocolate or even some tea. To her, travelling is first and foremost an opportunity to treat herself – and others – to food. She is so dominated by her own greed that she once broke her arm while trying clandestinely to pick her neighbour's peaches.

Without a moment's hesitation, she takes an almond cake, tastes it and immediately asks Mr Eskandari where she can buy them.

'Nowhere. It will be my pleasure to offer them to you,' Mr Eskandari replies swiftly, not losing sight of the apartment that needs finding nor the potential commission.

As she finishes her cake Nargess abruptly leans over towards the very chair Mr Eskandari is sitting on. She fingers the braid, gently pushing aside our caretaker's leg while he watches her every move in utter astonishment.

'*Agha* Morad,' she tackles the photographer boldly, 'what did you stick this braid on with? Saliva, I imagine!'

All eyes converge on Mr Eskandari's chair. He stands up and, telescoping all of his six-foot-four frame, bends over to follow the question of the braiding at close quarters. I know he won't give an opinion, he's in too much of a dilemma: on the one hand the photographers are meant to be tracing his son in Sweden, on the other Nargess could very well reward him with a handsome commission. He's caught in the crossfire. Any response would be dangerous, even detrimental.

Just then someone I really wasn't expecting comes into the room, Mr Upgrade in person, preceded by his powerful eau de cologne. He has come to remove the cables connecting my television to a satellite dish – which is hidden by the pots of religious offerings on the terrace of a true Gordafarid, a heroine who fears no one and lives on the nineteenth floor of my building.

The engineer says hello to my guests, smells the aroma of coffee, rubs his hands together and announces, 'Taking down a satellite dish in these conditions isn't really work, it's –'

'– a luxury!' Morad finishes his sentence for him.

Mr Sabeti, not very impressed by the photographer's verbal intrusion, comes over to the chair at the centre of everyone's attention.

'If you'll excuse me, madam,' he says, addressing my aunt, 'if you devoted a bit less time to your husband and a bit more to Nahal *khanoum*, then things like this –' he picks at the braid and pulls it off quite easily '– wouldn't happen.'

Morad gets up smartly and goes up to Mr Sabeti. I fear the worst: the two men could easily confront each other, right here, in my living room, the day before my departure.

My aunt is quick to intervene.

'What's this got to do with you?' she asks, raising her voice. 'None of you are upholsterers as far as I know! So sit down, have a cup of coffee and let the professionals deal with it!' Then she calls loudly, 'Mohtaram *khanoum*, more coffee please!'

Mr Eskandari, who is still standing, asks Mr Sabeti, 'Before you remove the cables could you upgrade the radio station for Iranians in Sweden?'

Hashem has just come back in with tea, not coffee. He hears these last words and says, '*Ey baba*, Mr Eskandari's still in Sweden. *Baradar*, my brother, forget Sweden, give it up. Come back to Iran, believe me, come back.'

Mr Eskandari lowers his eyes and silently folds away his crumpled old piece of paper with its random numbers, the only evidence that he once had a son.

'Come on, come into the library with me,' Mr Sabeti says to him. 'I'll do whatever you like. But before that I'd just like to ask this photographer: How come you turn up here one day as a furniture delivery man and then two days later in your supposed photo studio, Ec . . . I don't know what, you turn away customers and offer to help madam –' here he looks at me '– by getting hold of some doctor whose name I've forgotten? Mm? How come?'

I'm beginning to wonder whether this afternoon, which I've set aside for quiet goodbyes, isn't going to turn into a free-for-all fight.

Having been directly challenged and with the nerves in his neck threatening to snap with rage, Morad responds to the engineer, 'I had my doubts about you but not any more. I can see exactly what you are. Nahal *khanoum* could do with being more careful before she opens the door to just anybody.'

'Just anybody?' cries Mr Sabeti.

'Yes, just anybody – an informer, a spy.'

Trying to dampen the tension rapidly cranking up between the two men, I give a little laugh and say, 'A spy?'

'Yes, a spy!' replies Morad. 'Exactly! Does a spy have to have a tail and horns for people to recognise him?'

I go on laughing, although I don't feel like it at all. I think of my uncle and how he sees the destructive but all-powerful hand of English diplomacy everywhere, and ask, 'Who would you say Mr Sabeti is working for? The English, perhaps?'

'I wouldn't dare venture further in this vein,' Morad goes on, using peculiar diplomatic jargon. 'I will, however, permit myself to point out that this upgrading operation, which this dear gentleman has made his speciality, could be done by a child of eleven. Unless it's being used as a cover for other activities.'

Dr Bashiri then comes to the aid of the engineer who is actually due to upgrade a whole range of sports channels for him before the imminent withdrawal of all satellite dishes.

'*Agha* Morad,' he says, 'even though I'm very familiar with computers, I confess I have no idea how to carry out an upgrade. It's not child's play, I assure you.'

Feeling my blood pressure plummeting I swallow two almond cakes in quick succession and run to the kitchen to drink a large glass of sugared water. I find Mohtaram wrapping tins of coffee in plastic bags. She knows that, before I leave, I give her not only all the food but also beauty products, telephone cards, dried flowers, DVDs I've made . . . The reason she served tea instead of coffee earlier is something only I know. As the time for me to leave draws nearer she actually begins to think of these things as her own, and has absolutely no desire to waste her coffee by offering it to all and sundry.

I drink my sugared water. Mohtaram can see how uncomfortable I'm feeling.

'Just give me a minute, madam,' she says. 'I'll get rid of them all.'

With a wave of my hand I dissuade her (that's all I need), and go back into the living room. Mr Eskandari has stayed on his feet, still hoping to have his radio station for Iranian immigrants in Sweden upgraded. Nargess is sitting on the sofa, badgering Morad: 'You still haven't answered my question. What did you stick that braid on with?'

Distinctly more discreet and self-effacing than his colleague, Hassan answers in a measured voice, 'I don't have the honour of knowing you, madam –' (that makes him quite a rarity in Tehran) '– but I can guarantee that our wives, who are seamstresses and upholsterers, use the best products available in the city. They even have a contract with an Iran Air stewardess who supplies them with German thread every time she gets back from Frankfurt.'

Dr Bashiri nods his head knowledgeably and adds, 'German products are undeniably the best there are, particularly in household appliances and cars.' Then, probably thinking of the upcoming launch of Adidas in Iran, he goes on, 'Still, if I were you, I would have advised these upholsterers to import thread from France. Nahal *khanoum,* please correct me if I'm wrong but your husband's countrymen are not only the world leaders in fashion and cosmetics but also in sportswear, wouldn't you say?'

He winks at me, indicating the document on the table, the appendix to his market study whose sorry fate he doesn't know.

'We're not here to compare Mercedes and Peugeot,' Nargess interrupts him, 'but to sort out the future of this poor braid.'

'I didn't realise,' Mr Sabeti goes on rather tartly, 'that these photographers also exercised the delicate art of tapestry work.'

Knowing how much he loves coffee, I call Mohtaram with a degree of determination, 'Mohtaram, *khanoum!* A coffee for Mr Sabeti!'

She comes in straight away.

'I'm afraid there's no coffee left . . .' she says. '*May the evil eye spare you*, madam, you calculated how much you needed so well that I've literally just thrown the last tin in the bin.'

'Finished!' Hashem exclaims in English, clapping his hands together.

My aunt looks at him irritably: she loathes it when he unleashes English words on every topic. With a guilty face and drooping shoulders Hashem turns on his heel and goes back to the kitchen.

'Every time I come here,' Mr Sabeti starts again, addressing everyone except the two photographers whom he strenuously ignores, 'the smell of coffee goes to my head so quickly that I forget how monotonous my work is. I would never have thought it possible that my weakness for coffee would subject me to such a barrage of insults here.'

I feel like going into Mohtaram's bedroom, opening her various bags filled with nearly empty deodorants, dried-out mascaras, old hairbrushes with boar-hair bristles, melted chocolate and half-finished tins of coffee. Then I could extricate Mr Upgrade's beloved commodity and I personally could give him a cup of coffee. But I do nothing of the sort. I stay there on the long sofa created by my decorator friend – the one so taken with dead women's hands – and thereby avoid irritating Mohtaram on the eve of my departure.

'If you like drinking coffee so much then why don't you wait till you're back in peace and quiet at home and make yourself some of the good French coffee that madam gave you?' Morad suggests to Mr Sabeti.

'Because I'm waiting to drink the coffee madam gave you in peace and quiet at your home,' Mr Sabeti promptly replies.

'With permission from Mercedes, Peugeot and pure arabica coffee,' Nargess suddenly chimes in, still not giving up on her problem, 'I'd like to draw everyone's attention to the state of this braid.'

'Sabeti, *sarvaram*, my master, my house is yours,' says Morad, indifferent to Nargess's intervention, 'you will always be welcome there.'

The notion of hospitality, which is highly developed in Iranians, has just gained the upper hand over the absurd rivalry between the two men which was first declared in this very apartment six days ago.

'You are a master, Morad *djoun*,' replies Mr Sabeti.

'To mark this reconciliation, don't forget to invite us too,' suggests my aunt who always wants to be part of any gathering.

'Don't invite madam,' Dr Bashiri cuts in, knowing she won't go to this reconciliation anyway because she hasn't been anywhere since her husband's immobilisation. 'She won't come. Invite me instead.'

'You are all our guests,' Morad decrees. 'But not just for coffee, for a *tchelo* kebab. Hassan's kebab is unsurpassable!'

Mr Sabeti beckons the caretaker back into the library to upgrade the Iranian Swedish radio station. On his way past he gives a friendly tap on the shoulder to Morad and Hassan, the one standing, the other sitting down.

The photographers smile. The incident seems to be resolved. I can breathe.

The videophone rings and Mr Eskandari's stand-in announces from downstairs that Davar has arrived and is frustrated that the usual caretaker isn't there. Mohtaram tells him he is busy listening to Swedish radio and we can hear the stand-in's amazement all the way from the living room.

'Swedish radio?' he exclaims.

'Yes, Swedish radio,' Mohtaram replies. 'And I've got better things to do. Madam is leaving tomorrow and I seem to be spending all my time telling everyone what's going on.'

She must have switched off the videophone because we can no longer hear the stand-in's voice. Davar appears carrying a bunch of peonies. Mohtaram goes to let him in and her face lights up. By tomorrow evening these flowers will be gracing her 'open' (she uses this single English word to describe her American style open-plan kitchen).

I scold Davar because flowers are very expensive in Tehran.

'Spending all that money when you know I can only enjoy them for one night is such a waste!'

He doesn't say anything but sits himself down. I run to the kitchen to stop Mohtaram making him any coffee, which she would be perfectly capable of doing: my intellectual friend is far more than a lowly engineer, and the cost of the peonies would justify offering to the one the coffee she refused the other.

I thought as much. Mohtaram is already putting fresh water in the cafetière.

All at once I hear Kiara wailing in French. She's addressing Mr Sabeti who has had to interrupt the children's channels in order to upgrade the Swedish radio station.

I come out of the kitchen and, in the corridor, run into Mr Sabeti, pursued by my daughter and followed by Mr Eskandari.

'Madam, I must go,' says the latter, bowing his tall frame. 'I'll have to say goodbye now because I've been away from my post for too long.'

The irritation in his stand-in's voice must have reached his ears. The caretaker and the engineer end up back in the living room to say goodbye to each other. My aunt makes the most of their imminent departure by announcing that the time has come for everyone to leave. Ever since she was a young girl she has been unable to stay out after five o'clock in the afternoon.

'I don't even have to look at my watch,' she often says, 'but I can tell from an anxious feeling I get in the top of my stomach that it's gone five o'clock.'

I look at my watch: six-thirty — what torture for her! Out of habit and courtesy, I invite my guests to stay on longer but they all get up. My aunt leans over to Davar and invites him to dinner. He hesitates and I urge him on, reminding him he's only just arrived and saying that, as I have no choice but to spend my last evening with my uncle, it would be nice if he came too. Davar accepts. Nargess, who is like family and will therefore be joining us for supper, goes into the dining room and rips the braid off two more chairs.

'Aren't you ashamed to leave when you know full well this work's been badly done?' she exclaims. 'How can you?'

Morad and Hassan exchange looks.

'Nargess *khanoum*,' Hassan replies 'what about you, how could you possibly have thought we would leave without taking the chairs?'

'If that's the case,' Mr Sabeti chips in, 'let me nip up to the nineteenth floor to take down the satellite dish quickly and I'll come back and help you take the chairs downstairs.'

Dr Bashiri, Mr Eskandari and Davar also offer to help move the twelve chairs. Everyone's at it. Mr Eskandari is on duty this evening and he says his goodbyes once more. I kiss him, which would be strictly forbidden in the hallway on the ground floor, and take the opportunity to reassure him about his son: 'You can count on *agha* Morad and Hassan *agha*. They are men of their word. I know that.'

Morad comes over.

'One last request: could I see your passport?' he asks.

I go and get it, and show it to him. He opens it respectfully.

'Lovely photograph!' he cries. 'Really. Now every time you open it when you're escaping round the world you can think of your two photographer friends still imprisoned here.'

'I promise I'll go to the council offices to get your accommodation certificate as soon as I'm there,' I assure him.

'*Inshallah*,' says Mr Sabeti, who still hasn't gone up to the nineteenth floor. 'Nahal *khanoum*, I can't seem to move because I hate goodbyes but I just wanted to add that every time you switch from CNN to the BBC via Arte and Piwi without the picture scrambling, without some engineer having to secretly scale the side of the building every couple of days and end up bent double inside an old rice pot perched on the top floor in order to make a connection, spare a thought for your coffee-loving friend.'

I promise that too, then go into Mohtaram's bedroom, open one of her bags at random and take out a tin of coffee which I give to Mr Sabeti.

'Mohtaram *khanoum* has just found the last tin,' I tell him. 'It must be meant for you.'

He refuses to take it, probably afraid of unleashing some new coffee-related incident, but everyone encourages him, even Mohtaram who seems to have realised she went a bit too far. He takes the tin, overcome with emotion, and puts it in his briefcase.

'Sabeti *djoun*,' says Hassan, 'when you come to eat with us, don't forget your laptop please. There are two or three clusters of programmes which we can't seem to upgrade however hard we try.'

'*Beh rouy-e tcheshm*, I'll see to it myself, it'll be a pleasure.'

He gives them his mobile number and points out that he made a note of Morad's the day he went to Ecbatana studio with me to try and find Dâryoush.

Dr Bashiri shakes my hand, and that too would not have been possible downstairs. He points at the annexe to his market study and says, 'It's all in your hands now.'

'You can count on me, I'll get the whole package to the person in question as soon as I'm there.'

'Thank you for your discretion.'

Mr Sabeti and the two photographers eye him suspiciously. What secret understanding lurks beneath that 'discretion'? I'm happy I'm leaving: I wouldn't want to be a powerless witness to the latent hostilities between the four men again.

I go into my bedroom to touch up my make-up, and when I get back to the living room everyone has gone except for Mohtaram and Hashem who are busy clearing the coffee cups. I've decided not to give Mohtaram an explanation for opening her bag and taking out the coffee. 'Never complain, never explain,' as the Queen of England would say.

I rush downstairs and find Davar, Dr Bashiri, Mr Eskandari, Mr Sabeti and the two photographers all lumbering along the street to the Ecbatana studio with a couple of chairs. My aunt, Nargess, my daughter and I watch the caravan go into the studio and re-emerge empty-handed.

Hassan and Mr Sabeti come over to me and, at considerable personal risk, shake my hand. I give them a friendly pat on the back.

'Don't forget . . .' says Hassan.

'Don't forget . . .' adds Mr Sabeti.

'No, every time I open my passport, every time I zap channels, I'll think of you both.'

'*Ey baba*,' Dr Bashiri says, coming over to us, 'they've done their best to exhaust her this afternoon, now they're going to make her cry.'

'Come on, quickly, get in my car, your uncle's expecting us,' Nargess whispers to me.

'No, no,' Davar intervenes, 'I'm taking her.'

My aunt gets into Nargess's car and gesticulates to me to reapply my lipstick.

'Go with Davar but put a bit of make-up on. If you could see your face!'

I hear Mr Sabeti telling the caretaker he will come by tomorrow to take down the satellite dish once I have gone.

In Davar's car Kiara asks to listen to *Amor Amor* in Spanish, but Davar only has French easy-listening music. We are soon there and the car-locking exercise is not unlike Nargess's. We go up to my aunt's apartment where Samira, Masserat and Hamid welcome us with a tinge of sadness in their eyes. My aunt is sitting on the edge of my uncle's bed, telling him about the afternoon's events in profuse detail. My uncle warns me about the risks of supplying strangers with accommodation certificates, and Davar agrees with him. I can't see how Morad and Hassan could be members of a terrorist network, but don't say anything and nod approval of their vigilance.

I ask Davar my perennial question, 'What was the last sentence you translated today?'

He quotes from memory: 'I sat in the depths of a comfortable, sprung armchair which bore scars like an old soldier, offering up its torn arms for all to see, and displaying age-old pomade and hair-cream from friends' heads encrusted on its backrest. Opulence and poverty coupled naïvely on the bed, the walls, all around.'

He glances at my uncle's bed, the walls of the apartment and electric sockets marked by dirty fingerprints.

'Actually,' he adds, 'I couldn't get very far today. I spent my time trying to find out whether Deleuze wrote anything about Balzac.'

'And?'

'He wanted to with Félix Guattari, after their Kafka, but they both died before they could start.'

'So he didn't write anything about Balzac?'

'Just a few notes I haven't yet been able to lay my hands on.'

Mohtaram and Hashem come in and serve us supper. My aunt offers to spend the night in my apartment. It's what she used to do, in the past, the night before I went away with my mother and, later, on my own. I tell her Mohtaram was thrilled to be taking me to the airport. She knows, as we all do in fact, that Mohtaram likes going to the airport more than anything else and depriving her of this outing would be worse than taking one of her tins of coffee.

Davar offers to drop me off himself and I explain that Hashem, Mohtaram and myself have a faultless strategy: while I register the baggage and put it through all the checks, Mohtaram keeps Kiara busy in the airport concourse and Hashem parks the car. Then I go back to collect Kiara, kiss Mohtaram and shake Hashem's hand (at the airport we can even kiss men – it's tolerated there) before finally leaving.

Davar lets himself be persuaded: he won't come. Before leaving I sit at the foot of my uncle's bed and spend a long time silently massaging his legs. I can picture him in his youth, slim and elegant in his swimming trunks, greeting friends beside their huge pool. I can see him standing in Hermès deliberating between two pairs of John Lobb shoes. When I turn round to kiss him his face is wet with tears. I'm sure he's been picturing the same things. I get up, kiss my aunt and make her promise to come to Paris with my uncle for Kiara's birthday. Even though I know it's impossible I still do it because the hope of seeing each other again soon softens the blow of parting. I kiss Samira, Masserat and Hamid. Kiara is tired and refuses to kiss everyone. Hamid is in tears. So is my aunt.

'You really could have asked Dâryoush for your *kart-e melli*,' Nargess says critically in the lift.

'*Badan, badan*, another time.'

I kiss her and Davar – we're two storeys underground in my aunt's apartment block and it's eleven o'clock so we're unlikely to come across any informers. I get into Hashem's car with Kiara in my arms, and sit in the passenger seat. Ever since the Revolution Mohtaram has encouraged us to do this systematically so that Hashem doesn't look like a chauffeur. But my mother, who didn't want to be taken for a chauffeur's wife, didn't like it.

When we get home Mr Eskandari opens the car door for me and takes his crumpled piece of paper from his pocket. I reassure him yet again: 'In three weeks the photographers might have their visa and be free to go to Sweden.'

I go up to my room and get Kiara undressed. She wants to be on the plane now. I close my eyes and think of all the people I've met and made such strong connections with, people who have done their best to help me so that — at the end of the day — I could leave them.

Tuesday

A black metal gate opens and my husband, my daughter and I walk along a driveway lined with ancient olive trees with as many trunks as they have branches. A dark-skinned local, who seems to be wearing a Mexican hat, explains in Spanish that they were planted there, illegally, four hundred and fifty years ago. We are swallowed up by the green of the grass and the green of the olive trees on either side. Occasionally three young blonde women and my daughter's nanny appear. We go into a tumbledown little church where a glass case houses a statue of Christ which, the local informs us, grows one centimetre every year so that the glass cage has to be extended. My daughter lights a candle and rings a bell.

The alarm clock says it's four in the morning. I have to get up. We're leaving today. My bag is ready except I just need to hide the caviare in my socks and slip them into my old trainers. Once that's done I wake Kiara and get her dressed despite an avalanche of sundry protests. Mohtaram has already made breakfast. I drink my last cup of coffee but Kiara refuses to eat.

We're ready to leave. Mohtaram is standing by the front door of the apartment with a copy of the Koran and a glass of water. Kiara and I walk beneath the Koran as she brandishes it in the air, we kiss it and go out. Mohtaram spills the water in our tracks: may our leaving run as smoothly as this flowing water.

Hashem takes our bags downstairs while Mohtaram, who knows how worried I am about the caviare, recites a prayer over the red suitcase, the one with the delicious cargo. When we get downstairs we find Mr Eskandari is already up, and he kisses me once again – there's no one in the hallway to see. Hashem's car is parked outside and we climb into it. As usual, Mohtaram offers me the front seat. I don't argue even though, with my daughter in my arms, it would be much more comfortable for me to sit in the back. The car sets off and we drive past the Ecbatana studio where I notice, in the half-light, my great string of chairs taking up a ridiculous amount of space inside.

'Let's hope they haven't changed their minds,' Mohtaram and Hashem say simultaneously.

I don't say anything. In three hours' time the chair problem won't be mine to worry about any more.

We get to the airport quickly. Since the Revolution I've found, as have millions of others, that all arrivals and departures go hand in hand with endless fears and anxieties. I have awful memories of the Islamic regime's early years: I once slipped a ring worth a hundred euros into my suitcase and it was found by a customs officer, and for that one small ring I not only missed my flight but was subjected to a revolutionary trial on the spot.

The airport is also one of the places where intellectuals who preach non-violence can be arrested, accused of being 'a threat to national security'. That's why some old granny from the provinces who has never shown the least interest in politics can turn up here and find she's refused permission to leave Iranian soil. Having missed her flight – to, say, Sweden – she will then be shuttled from one organisation to another for a couple of months. She could easily end up at the passport office in Yaft Abad with a chicken hidden under her chador as a thank you for one Lieutenant Mokhtarpour for untangling the problem which may have originated, as often happens, in the similarity of a name.

Mohtaram, Hashem and I put into action the plan we have been using since the birth of my daughter. Hashem takes the bags from the boot of the car, goes and finds a (skinny and toothless) old porter and heads for the car park. Mohtaram takes Kiara in her arms while I go through the first checkpoint, reserved for women. One female inspector stands and checks my ticket while two others, sitting down, assess how Islamic my outfit is. I get through the booth, one ordeal over, and meet up with the porter in the passenger area. I promise him a handsome reward if he manages to get me through the first visual check without any problems. He asks me a question in Turkish. I don't know what to say and, for the first time in my life, regret that I'm not from Azerbaijan. I hope the customs men, inspectors, porters and perhaps all of the airport personnel are natives of this province in north-west Iran which shares a border with Turkey.

The old porter puts my bags on the conveyor belt. My heart thumps as they go through the visual check: will the (Turkish?) inspector spot my caviare? The porter mumbles a few words to him, actually in Turkish, and picks up my bags from the far end of the conveyor belt. I've just sailed through the second ordeal. Now I come to a man who has it in his power to open up my bags and, for reasons known only to himself, stop me proceeding to check-in. He is sitting on a stool, his hair is parted exaggeratedly far over on the left-hand side, like the Director of the Theatres Association, his shirt is hermetically buttoned and he has the most astonishingly Islamic shaving technique, sporting exactly three days' worth of stubble.

Right now I'm beginning to regret not only my ignorance of the Turkish language but the fact that I forgot to copy out my aunt's prayer, a prayer in Arabic which specialises in opening doors and making obstacles melt away. I know it starts with something like *fadja alna* but don't know the rest. I settle for repeating the words *fadja alna* several times and manage to get through the third ordeal without attracting the attention of this man in civilian clothes who holds my fate in his hands.

I now head over to the Iran Air desks. For once there's barely a queue. I think of the conversation sparked off by my friends in Paris whenever travelling to Iran is mentioned.

'Which company are you flying with?' an exiled friend might ask me.

'I don't know yet, probably Iran Air.'

'Forget Iran Air. They haven't updated their fleet for thirty years,' says a young man who seems very well informed on the aeronautical industry.

'I fly from Paris to Dubai with Emirates and spend a night in one of the city's palace hotels. The next day I swim in the pool on the fiftieth floor of the hotel and spend half an hour in the spa's float tank, then I take an Emirates flight to Tehran,' explains a thrusting young businessman who I imagine is snowed under with work.

'If my calculations are accurate, it takes you two days to make a journey of four and a half hours,' I say.

'Yes, but he's guaranteed to arrive alive, even if he does lose twenty-four hours – and not a couple of days, as you've just claimed. Nahal,' the aeronautical expert entreats me, 'you should stop using Iran Air too.'

'You're right. My brother, who ran Iran Air before the Revolution and was personally responsible for buying all its aircraft, keeps telling me the same thing.'

The exiled friend who no longer goes to Iran, the so-called aeronautical expert and the *über*-busy businessman (still all in Paris) chorus at me: 'Will you now admit that it's really dangerous to fly Iran Air?'

'Yes.'

'Have we finally managed to persuade you?'

'Yes.'

'So who are you going to fly with, then?' the exiled friend asks to close the conversation.

'With Iran Air,' I say every time, bringing an end to the discussion.

It's my turn now. I know that my baggage exceeds the allowance by twenty kilos. The porter whispers a few more words in Turkish to the Iran Air employee weighing my bags. I'm about to go over the only words I know from the prayer for good 'outcomes' once more when I realise the man in question is meekly attaching Paris–Orly tickets to my bags. He checks my passport and my daughter's, gives me our boarding passes and wishes me a good flight. I've just passed the fourth ordeal (a material one this time) with a sense of jubilation due to my choice of airline – not Air France whose zero-tolerance policy would have required me to pay at least two hundred euros.

I ask the porter how much I owe him. He wants twenty thousand *tomans*, the equivalent of twenty euros, when I have four bags and the official rate per bag is twenty centimes. I protest; I only want to give him ten euros which is more than enough. He reminds me that he saved my caviare and reduced my excess baggage payment to nothing. He's right there, but I don't want to give in – this last stay in Iran must have hardened me.

'Fifteen thousand and not one *toman* more.'

'Twenty thousand and not one *toman* less.'

'Seventeen thousand and that's it,' I say, taking out my purse.

'Put your purse away quickly. Pay me at the exit when you've picked up your daughter.'

I turn round and walk back past the man sitting on his stool, the inspectors overseeing the conveyor belt and the women in the clothing check booth. In the main concourse I meet up with Mohtaram, Hashem and Kiara, and pay the porter. He counts his seventeen thousand *tomans* a couple of times, grumbles to himself but eventually leaves. I kiss Mohtaram and even Hashem, and ask them to look after my aunt and uncle.

At the last moment, before I go back into the clothing booth, Mohtaram says, 'The last time I saw madam' – she means my mother – 'was by this doorway. I massaged her feet all through the night before she travelled because her bones were hurting her so much.' Then Mohtaram rests her head on my shoulder and adds, 'She went in there and I never saw her again.'

My mother left Tehran for the last time in April 2001 and died in Paris in December of the same year. I can feel Mohtaram's tears on me, and stroke her head through her scarf.

'*May God spare her soul,*' says Hashem. 'I was here too.'

'What about me?' asks Kiara.

'You weren't born yet,' I tell her.

'Madam left so that you could come. We waited so eagerly for you,' Mohtaram adds.

'Where was I?'

I pick her up in my arms and promise to explain where she was before she was born.

'Promise you will, swear you will?' she asks.

'I promise and I swear.'

I shake Hashem's hand, kiss Mohtaram once more and tell her that her son Hamid can have my friend's computer if he likes.

'But it doesn't work,' Hashem chips in.

'He's always got something to say about everything,' Mohtaram says of her husband. 'What do you want madam to do about it now, an hour before she leaves? Do you want her to get it mended?'

I stop myself offering to cover the cost of repairs to the computer, knowing full well that, armed with power of attorney, my aunt will do it in my name anyway. I go into the women's booth with Kiara in my arms. The three inspectors – one standing and two sitting – don't bother checking anything. They must have recognised me too, like their counterparts in the Central Passport Office. How do they do that? I have no idea.

I get to the man sitting on his stool and try to make myself small and inconspicuous. Kiara is talking to me in French but I reply in Persian: now is not the time to attract this man's attention. I get on to the escalator and when we're half-way up Kiara asks to go back down. She wants to get on to it without my help. That's the price I pay for antenatal stimulation and Montessori school: she wants to do everything herself. If I left her to her own devices she could quite easily catch a taxi and get to the airport by herself.

I go back down, still trying not to arouse the curiosity of the man on the stool, the one who could, at any moment and for reasons known only to himself stop me leaving the country (I mean, going all the way down the up escalator could be deemed a subversive act).

Kiara gets on and I follow her. At the top we come to passport control. I slide my precious passport which has caused me so many problems under the glass window. The officer taps a few keys on his computer while I think of all the people who have been arrested or turned away at this very stage. He checks my photograph and suddenly, although I couldn't say why, I remember the smell of cigarettes on Morad's hands as he took my chin to alter the angle of my head for my ID photo.

After a few minutes the man eventually stamps my passport. Now it's Kiara's turn. I lift her up to the level of the counter. She too is treated to computer checks and a long wait before the thud of the stamp on her passport, the fifth and decisive ordeal. Kiara grabs her passport, the first she has had in her life, and wants to hold on to it. She clasps it tightly: perhaps she can tell it's a rare and precious thing.

I trust her – this isn't the moment to launch into a whole new passport saga.

We get to the hand-luggage check and I mumble the first words of my 'door opening' prayer again: *fadja alna*. In my bag I'm carrying a Rolex watch for my best friend's daughter, a birthday present from her grandmother. Thirty years ago the same inspectors (no, their mothers) would have stopped me for fraudulently taking our national property out of the country. My bag goes on to the conveyor belt. As she prods beneath my arms, one of the women asks me about the contents of the box.

'A Rolex watch,' I say.

'A real one?' she asks, patting along my thighs.

Her colleague is scanning the screen and says, 'A fake wouldn't have this packaging.'

Kiara puts her backpack on the conveyor belt and waits for the inspector's verdict. Not only is she allowed through but she's entitled to a '*Mashallah*, may God save you from the evil eye.' Sixth ordeal over. We queue up for the final check, the one for visas, carried out by a member of the Iran Air staff. Kiara has a French passport and gets through this last test easily while, with my Iranian passport devoid of any visas, I risk being refused the right to board the flight. So I discreetly produce my French passport. The Iran Air employee compares the two passports and finally allows me down on to the sloping walkway to the bus. Seventh ordeal.

In the bus I list the seven ordeals that Iran's legendary hero, Rostam, had to confront to save his native country; I also list the seven valleys that Attar's birds had to cross in order to become themselves at last, to reach the bird-king, Simorgh: among them were the valley of love, the valley of terror, the valley of death . . .

We start climbing the stairs up to the plane, Kiara in front and me behind. She shows the air hostess her boarding card and I do the same. We find our seats.

The hostesses wear scarves topped with a head-dress, long tunics and wide trousers. The plane really does seem to date back to the 1970s but I immediately drive away any fears of mechanical failure as best I can: Iran Air's pilots are the best in the world. You need only witness one of their landings to be utterly convinced. Why do they have this reputation? I don't know.

The hostesses are now doing their passenger count, the

doors are closing. Guards in civilian clothes take their seats dotted about the cabin. You can spot them by their distinctive partings far down on the left-hand side of their heads and, of course, their lack of luggage. The head of the cabin crew, a woman, announces, 'With our respects to the soul of the Islamic Republic's founder, Imam Khomeyni, and our respects to the immaculate souls of our martyrs, Captain Massoumi and his crew would like to welcome you on board. Our flight time to Paris is estimated at five hours . . .'

Soon after that the plane takes off and flies over the chain of mountains round Tehran. I point it out to my daughter and, as I always do, ask what it's called.

'Alborz,' she says.

I look at the Alborz mountains which stood over me as I was born, and take off my scarf.

www.virago.co.uk

virago

To find out more about Nahal Tajadod and other Virago authors, visit:
www.virago.co.uk

Visit the Virago website for:

- Exclusive features and interviews with authors, including Margaret Atwood, Maya Angelou, Sarah Waters and Nina Bawden

- News of author events and forthcoming titles

- Competitions

- Exclusive signed copies

- Discounts on new publications

- Book-group guides

- Free extracts from a wide range of titles

PLUS: subscribe to our free monthly newsletter